DOUBLE-TRACKING

DOUBLE-TRACKING

TRACKING

Studies in Duplicity

ROSANNA MCLAUGHLIN

LITTLE ISLAND PRESS

in collaboration with Carcanet

First published in Great Britain in 2019 by
Little Island Press / Carcanet
Alliance House, 30 Cross Street
Manchester M2 7AQ
www.carcanet.co.uk

A CIP catalogue record for this book is
available from the British Library.
ISBN 9978 0 99570 522 7

Book design by Andrew Latimer
Printed in Great Britain by SRP Ltd, Exeter, Devon

Supported using public funding by the National Lottery
through Arts Council England.

CONTENTS

for M.C.H.

I
THE ORIGINS OF DOUBLE-TRACKING

On the throne of the world, any delusion can become fact.
Gore Vidal

A RUDE AWAKENING

People have been talking about it. The little café, housed in a former upholsterer's tucked away behind the high street, is not the sort of place you'd ever expect to find among the discount stores and the chicken shops on the Walworth Road. It's a beautiful morning, cold and crisp and clear, the sky shot through with such pretty notes of pink and blue that you can almost taste the sherbet. I button up my jacket, lace up my boots and head out with breakfast in mind. How masonic, I think, looking up at the sign above the door, on to which a pair of callipers has been painted in an antiquarian shade of green, and cross the threshold beholden to the glamour of Olde Labour.

Inside I notice with relief the flour-dusted breads, placed on a rack in distressed wooden crates like a display hoiked from a local history museum: Sculleries Through the Ages. Who could have anticipated how difficult it would be to get a decent loaf around here? And standing in line I casually listen in to the people in front of me discussing the state of British politics... the sheer poverty of compassion these days... a conversation the entire café seems to be nodding along to, customers, furniture, food and all, and which, combined with the sound of frothing milk and the Johnny Cash record playing in the background, thrum along to a tune so familiar that the man beside the polenta cake has begun to tap it out on the counter. *Tum-tu-tum-tum, tum-tu-tum-tum* go his thumb and forefinger, *I'm stuck in Folsom Prison, and time keeps draa-gin on*, goes Johnny Cash, and he's happy to serve his time, tip-tapping those fingers, snug in the atmosphere of the small, over-crowded room like a baby in a blanket.

And wait we must, because everyone knows that in 2019 it takes at least ten minutes for a decent cup of coffee to materialise, time enough for the baristas, those proxy craftsmen of the flat-white epoch, to scribble orders on tickets, grind boutique beans, check weights and temperatures, clean mechanical protuberances, bash metal jugs, flick tea-towels over shoulders and hair from out of eyes, and most importantly of all, scribe their ephemeral signatures in milk and caffeine. Wait, until I am perched on the edge of a wooden work bench with a bitter lukewarm heart dissolving on my lips.

I unlock my phone, and allow my neural pathways to slacken as I cast my mind adrift on the backwaters of the *Guardian* online. *I'm not cold, I just don't have any romantic feelings*, swish, *Was Theresa May's Frida Kahlo bracelet a political statement?*, swish, until finally, and entirely at the mercy of the neo-liberal Fates, who swapped the Moira's golden threads for the digital algorithm (and a large portion of San Francisco's bay area), I arrive at an article detailing the optimum way to incorporate workwear into the reader's wardrobe. 'The trick, perhaps, is the softy-softly approach – take two components rather than head-to-toe', advises the writer. 'Otherwise, well, you risk venturing into fancy dress, and that will ruin the "worker look" for everyone.'

The worker look? My morning cruise through the canals of Sunday journalism is disturbed by the thought of the builders less than a mile from where I'm sat, working on a private housing development the size of a small town that's currently rising from the site of a razed council estate like a free-market phoenix. Ruined, for everyone? Surely nobody among the rebar and the concrete mixers is in any danger of over-doing a French canvas jacket by pairing it with a vintage boiler suit, two sartorial choices flatly absent among the tracksuit bottoms and the neon tabards.

The discordance between labour chic and labour proper increases when a waitress arrives with breakfast, placing on the table a single slice of brittle toast with half an avocado on top of it, accompanied by an unidentified sprig of bitter greenery. Sensing that there's been some sort of mistake – for I distinctly remember there being a whole host of ingredients – I cast my eyes in the direction of the chalkboard. But there it is. 'Artisan sourdough, smashed avocado, cold-pressed olive oil, garden salad. 8.' Artisan? Are the couple to my right discussing their plans for a loft extension not a graphic designer and an events manager but a wheelwright and a cooper, employed as sleeper agents for an ancient guild, deep, *deep* undercover, eating bowls of pottage cunningly disguised as granola? Things get worse when the sourdough shatters beneath my cutlery propelling a large shard of crust onto the floor, where it's pounced upon by a sheepdog miles away from anything vaguely resembling livestock and with nothing better to do than round up crumbs. *£8 for this dry slice of phoney rusticism?*

It's an observable truth that today's middle-classes are never so politically roused as when they feel that they, personally, are being shafted – a pathology of privilege most explicit in the cases of those people who, having flown halfway around the world to luxuriate at the expense of someone else's relative economic hardship, pride themselves on holding to account any driver, waiter, stall-holder, or guesthouse receptionist whom they suspect is not charging them 'local prices'; the claim to righteousness, to the belief that you are an outsider to a corrupt global order and a thorn in the side of the establishment, may be as slender as a midge's mandibles, but if challenged, it is likely to prove just as irascible.

Through newly disaffected eyes, the interior of the café takes on a distinctly unflattering appearance. The stripes, the sailor stripes! Everywhere I turn, long-sleeved and short-sleeved, tucked into jeans cut with hooks to hang non-existent hammers, peeping out from underneath yellow fishermen's macs, and an array of jackets that look like they've been pinched from the lockers of timber merchants, green grocers, and bin men sometime in the 1930s... Even that plump, blonde toddler in the corner is wearing them. I really ought to be above picking on children, but all the same, such ubiquity makes it hard to differentiate between the two-year-olds and the forty-two-year-olds. They all look so *coddled*, dressed in mix-and-match uniforms, ready for a play date at the local One O'clock Club.

And looking down I am ashamed to see that I, too, am ringed in white and navy. What is this pattern, that winds about my body? I, who have never scrubbed a deck or mended rigging, who have never signed away my youth on a bockety promise of a career, national duty and a sense of belonging? In the throes of ecstatic clarity, I pull the shirt from over my head, grab a loaf from the wooden rack – wisely opting for rye, owing to its unrivalled density – and launch it at the window, before leaving hot-cheeked and half-naked, but free at last.

Except of course I don't.

I eat the remains of my toast, stroke the dog that got the rest of it, and politely thank the waitress, wondering all the while whether it's time to move on to pastures new. South of here, perhaps – where there are still at least half a dozen functioning workshops and garages that haven't been bought up by the junior population of the home counties, leafy renegades who have arrived in the city on a quest to convert commercial properties into little Bohemias, places where pudding can be eaten before dinner, glitter-wrestling parties are a distinct possibility, DIY saunas are obligatory and *Where the Wild Things Are* is tantamount to a political manifesto. South, where the breakfasts are cheaper, and for the time being the stripes are fewer, but if you happen to know the right places, the coffee – that talisman of class, that line in the sand, that marker of Pierre Bordieu's *habitus* – is equally distinguished.

So the wheels of gentrification turn. But on such an occasion, when a tear opens up in the fabric of things, and the theatre of authenticity reveals itself, I found myself compelled to ask: what is this fantasy of hardship and labour endemic to those parts of the city catering to the rise of affluence, the empire of the flat-whites, draining neighbourhoods of colour, and leaving in their wake a mild-mannered army dressed in Breton stripes and vintage labouring apparel? What is this love of the workshop, the jailhouse, the farm, and the forces, which has caused a swathe of the population to tether their identities to the gates of histories and industries that they will never enter? I give to you, the superlative product of middle-class cognitive dissonance, the *double-tracker.*

AN INTRODUCTION

The term double-tracking was coined by the writer Tom Wolfe in 1970 as a means of describing the state of duplicity required to get ahead in the arts. To double-track is to be both: counter-cultural and establishment, rich and poor, Maldon Sea Salt of the earth, a bum with the keys to a country retreat, an exotic addition to the dinner table who still knows how to find their way around the silverware. Beneath the double-tracking coat of arms, in which a bindle crosses paths with a spear of asparagus, Pablo Picasso's immortal words fill the scroll: 'I want to be a poor man, with lots of money.'

It was a motto Picasso mastered, holding tight to the mythos of the garret, even as he sauntered through the hallways of MoMA. Charles Baudelaire was a fan. 'By "man of the world", I mean a man of the whole world, a man who understands the world and its mysterious customs', he wrote in praise of the painter Constantin Guys, connoisseur of common street scenes, proto-flâneur, and ideal embodiment of the Baudelaireian modern man. 'By "artist", I mean a specialist, a man tied to his palette like a serf to the soil.' The sculptor Carl Andre still abides by it. Having declared that he'd resigned from the middle-classes in the mid-nineteen fifties, Andre took to calling himself an 'artworker', and ditched his shirt and tie in favour of a pair of workman's overalls, an outfit he has worn henceforth as a token of his implacable saltiness – whether drinking champagne at Max's Kansas City, on trial for the murder of his wife Ana Mendieta, or in recent years, posing for *The New Yorker* in his Manhattan apartment.

'The contemporary art world', wrote Robert Katz, of the conflicted sense of identity prevalent among Andre's milieu, 'in spite of its ceaseless, spellbinding tango with bohemia, tangoed no place else but in one of the better-appointed ballrooms of the middle-class, to which it grudgingly belongs. Few other human endeavours have gone so far to feign aloofness while spending so much energy in educating the manners, easing the stress, and warming the hearts, brightening the environment, guarding the heritage, protecting the future, abiding the caprice, stroking the conscience, feeding the fantasy, sharing the dreams, and consuming every crumb of largess of the object of disdain.' Among the owners of those better-appointed ballrooms, the fantasy of the peon has long been catnip to the squire. So much so, that an artist may find their biography cast by the wayside should a more titillating narrative present itself. According to the art dealer Jeffrey Deitch, when Jean-Michel Basquiat had his first solo show at Annina Nosei gallery in New York in 1982, he was 'likened to the wild boy raised by wolves, corralled into Annina's basement and given nice clean canvases to work on instead of anonymous walls'. Nobody paid any mind to the fact that Basquait was well-schooled in the manners and modalities of art, that as a child, as the art historian Cora Gilroy-Ware has pointed out, his mother signed him up as a junior member of the Brooklyn Museum, and took him on regular visits to MoMA to view *Water Lilies* and *Guernica*.

Norman Mailer took double-tracking beyond the pale with his 1957 essay 'The White Negro', in which he declared that 'a new breed' of white adventurer had emerged, 'who drifted out at night looking for action with a black man's code to fit their facts'. Mailer named this adventurer the 'hipster', and he was, to all intents and purposes, an avatar for the writer himself: a young, white, psychically frustrated North American, entranced by a reverie of his own creation, in which the black man featured as a libidinous, semi-psychopathic, marginalised, anti-establishment idol – a figure designed, one can only assume, to provide an exciting alternative to the mundane comfort of his own existence. The hipster was not content with appreciating African American culture. He wanted to possess it, too, so much so that he argued it was a part of his own physiology. 'He had absorbed the existentialist synapses of the Negro', Mailer wrote, a feat apparently achieved by listening to Jazz and adopting an African American vocabulary, and 'for practical purposes could be considered a White Negro'. What the hipster had to bring to the party beyond racial stereotypes is unclear, though whiteness was certainly not on offer.

And so it is, that Norman Mailer provides lesson number one in the fine art of double-tracking: It's a one-way street.

For the British, George Orwell's *Down and Out in Paris and London* (1933) continues to prove instructive. In the process of writing it, Orwell unwittingly produced the blue print for today's gap-year industry. After chronicling his time tramping around the doss houses of Europe, no self-respecting eighteen-year-old would ever admit to spending their money on anything so transparently hedonistic as a lengthy luxury holiday. So dawned an unusual era for the travel industry, a time of customers willing to part with their money to sleep in shepherd's huts, spend time in historic slums, and experience the once-in-a-lifetime pleasure of working as a farm-hand. Indeed, what distinguishes the traveller from the tourist is key to understanding the double-tracking state of mind. Today's traveller is the tourist's embarrassed progeny, ashamed of their parents' laminated itinerary, beige money belt and sensible walking sandals. But rather than considering the root of this embarrassment – how narrow our sense of normalcy, how patently foolish we appear beyond familiar terrain, how ugly inequality – the traveller quells their anxiety of righteousness by engaging, *a la* Mailer, in an immersive type of role play. Just as jogging bottoms and neon tabards do nothing to excite the vintage workwear aficionado, the present day is often of little interest to the traveller, who side-steps any potential conflict with reality by seeking out those places designed to give the impression of standing still – communities that appear as if unchanged by the passage time, regardless of whether large parts of the coastline are rented out by foreign owners on Airbnb – causing a market to blossom in local trinkets dreamed up in distant factories, and unbeaten tracks that are nevertheless chartered in international guide books, over which at least five accountants out for drinks on Clapham High Street on any given Saturday could reminisce.

It is for the traveller, then, to deliver lesson number two: The double-tracker hankers after an image of authenticity that has been modelled with their patronage in mind, thus their activities extend beyond the realm of cultural appropriation, and into cultural invention.

Tom Wolfe located the apex of double-tracking as the art world, but today, it's a corner-stone of the middle-classes, and a full-blown commonplace of contemporary life. At root, it's a state of mind born of an ambivalent relationship to privilege, that, when perfected, allows those with financial resources the economic benefits of leaning right, and the cultural benefits of leaning left. 'Truly successful double-tracking,' wrote Wolfe, delivering lesson number three, 'requires the artist to be a sincere and committed performer in both roles.' It curls around the vocal chords of private school alumni as they drop their consonants, sprays the can of legally sanctioned graffiti on the side of the pop-up container shopping mall, and tones the cores of sweaty executives attending weekly parkour classes, prancing about the concrete furniture of housing estates they do not live on. It even sprinkles the heady mix of suspense and elation over those who adopt the time-honoured act of coming-out, stepping out of the closet and into the warm embrace of acceptance, when revealing to their friends that they own the squat they live in, or that their family inheritance was acquired by dubious means (arms sales or oil fortunes, anyone?). It is present in food and drink establishments with names like Urchin Wines, Vagabond Coffee Grinders, Favela Chic, The Begging Bowl, Revolution, The Job Centre (yes, it does exist) and The Workers' Café, where the only work done is on laptops; work benches used as coffee shop furniture; Hessian sacks placed on coffee shop furniture in lieu of cushions; warehouse conversions; intentionally distressed brick walls; expensive local street food markets that replace markets already selling food to locals, thereby replacing the locals too; pretend dive-bars; modern speakeasies; the serving of cocktails out of old jam jars and tin cans; craft beer; artisan quiche; vintage vegetable crates; ye olde fantasies of historical butchers, bakers and greengrocers;

the repackaging of old filing cabinets and other depressing items of office furniture as luxury period design pieces; the finding of ways to rephrase subletting your room and moving back in with your parents in order to avoid paying rent (e.g. 'I am giving up my possessions and going on a six-month retreat'); 'pop-ups', and other straightforward business ventures that fashion themselves on fugitive, DIY happenings; workwear jeans; anything made by Carhartt; vintage French canvas jackets; You Must Create's Delinquents shirt (£145) and Factory coat (£395); the entire contents of the chain Labour and Wait, purveyor of chore coats (£140), luxury leather tool belts (£55), pieces of rope tied in knots for nautical-themed cleaning activities (£18), specially procured vintage toilet brushes, and all manner of enamel cooking equipment, so customers can experience the joys of the WW1 mess kit without the bother of the trenches; gourmet fast-food vendors with names like Honest Burger, which pander to a fantasy of brute, triple fried, cave-dwelling masculinity, while maintaining a certain class distinction (this is not McDonalds, after all); the paleo diet, luxury barbecue equipment, and other quirks of the urban caveman movement, including running around the city barefoot (or buying shoes that approximate the experience); Dior Sauvage; David Cameron's £25,000 shepherd hut; fake mud with which to spray the wheel arches of your four by four, should you not actually live on a farm; coffee table books of prison tattoos; Mick Jagger, a grammar school boy from Kent, singing the blues and attempting to dance like James Brown (and looking 'about as sexy as a pissing toad', as Truman Capote put it); pre-work military bootcamps; wilderness weekends; urban foraging; farmers' markets; lumberjack shirts; fishermen's raincoats; knitting your own fisherman's jumper using wool that costs the same price as a small boat; and, of course, the ubiquitous sailor stripe.

Radical Chic, after all, is only radical in Style;
in its heart it is part of Society and its traditions.
Tom Wolfe

In every double-tracker's wardrobe, in the vicinity of every item of furniture made from reclaimed pallets, you will likely find at least one stripy t-shirt. The Breton stripe first appeared in 1858 as a uniform for low-ranking French seamen, worn as an undergarment visible through the V-neck of a sailor's suit, each bar representing one of Napoleon's naval victories. A few decades later, it became popular among musicians working the Parisian bal-musette circuit, late-night dances with a reputation for sleaze which attracted the attention of wealthy Parisians, keen for a brush with the city's underbelly. Nightclub proprietors who got wise to the mores of the bourgeoisie took to staging phoney police raids for the excitement of their upmarket visitors. The fortunes of the Breton shirt would change forever when it was picked up by Gabrielle Bonheur 'Coco' Chanel, Nazi collaborator and perennial darling of the fashion industry, who included it in her 1917 range. Chanel repackaged the seamen's underwear for the all-hands-on-deckchairs contingent of the French Riviera, and in the process, made the striped t-shirt a staple of haute worker chic. Jean Genet drenched it in 'those knock-out body fluids: blood, sperm, tears', in his 1947 nautical slasher fantasy, *Querelle of Brest*, Picasso was rarely seen out of one, and the beats took to the stripes like the empire took to tea (that is, with unselfconscious gusto). Since the 1980s, the fashion designer Jean Paul Gaultier has fully depended on them. 'I wore them everywhere, even with a tuxedo for gala evenings', he reflected on the early years of this love affair, hanging a nonpareil example of mixed fortunes couture in the double-tracking wardrobe.

Over the coming centuries the canny proprietors of the bal-musette nightclubs morphed into business graduates with a penchant for immersive theatre, and an eye for hawking the misfortunes of others. The result: a 'pop-up' bar named Alcotraz that opened in 2017 on London's Brick Lane, which advertised, at a cost of thirty pounds, the opportunity for customers to arrive at a fake prison with bottles of spirits they themselves have purchased in advance, dress up in orange jumpsuits, hide said booze inside a hollowed-out bible, 'sneak' it past an actor dressed as a warden, and drink made-to-order cocktails out of tin cans while sitting inside 'real metallic cells'. I contacted the company to enquire about the appeal of the US penitentiary system. 'Hi Rosanna', came the reply, from a correspondent who signed off 'the Warden of Alcotraz!'. 'As I am sure you will appreciate, managing these inmates takes up a great deal of my time.' In the theatre of hard knocks, corpsing is clearly not an option. 'Having personally always been fascinated about Alcatraz Island, its inmates and stories, the intention of the pop-up bar is not to romanticize imprisonment but rather create an engaging experience for guests that gently opens the door to worlds only seen by most in fiction.' The benevolence does not stop there. 'The company behind Alcotraz, Inventive Productions, is also working to see how it can partner with local communities to promote rehabilitation initiatives and encourage a greater learning of what took place within Alcatraz.'

Ah, outreach! So often turned to as a cultural hand-sanitiser, a Jersey account through which all manner of dubious gains can pass, returned for inspection looking as clean as a pair of pink-bottomed cherubs snuggling in a Moses basket. One wonders whether the learning encouraged will also extend to the current US penitentiary system, where black men are five times more likely to be incarcerated than their white counterparts, labour is a legal requirement, and, as part of this modern-day servitude in the land of the free, the average prisoner earns ninety cents an hour, yielding annual profits of over 500 million dollars and more still in tax breaks for white men including, but not limited to, the CEOs of Starbucks, Whole Foods and British Petroleum. Inventive Productions are currently working on 'Project number 2'. Where to go from here? A shooting range in a mock-up nursery, where customers smuggle weapons past child actors, complimented by the rolling out of a gun control advocacy programme in the local estates? A day spa set in a flooded Ganges Delta, and an accompanying lecture series on the perils of waste and global warming staged for the benefit of the citizens of Dhaka?

One thing of which you can be fairly certain is that it won't be set inside a South Asian mine – among most perilous workplaces going – because that idea has already been taken. In the summer of 2017, I spent an evening at a bar named Mineority in the Indian city of Pune. 'Mineority is a fun and young concept for the miners, their loved ones and the mine-owners' read an introduction on the menu, placed on the tables of a venue that catered to precisely zero of the advertised clientele, but instead offered the city's white-collar workers an opportunity to pose for selfies wearing yellow hard hats, standing in front of murals of filthy and exhausted men, surrounded by empty canary cages. Among the range of drinks on offer were '3 Penicillium Shots' – so named because 'miners in the oldest copper mines of India were treated with penicillium to prevent Tetanus' – and 'Coal Blooded' – for the appetising reason that 'miners and mining engineers working inside the mines suffered from coal dust accumulated in the respiratory system and in the blood'. Alcotraz and Mineority teach an important lesson to anyone wishing to perfect the art of being both: despite all evidence to the contrary, it is incumbent upon the double-tracker to consider your caprices benevolently motivated.

By the early twenty-first century the reign of the double-tracker had extended across the globe, but where might we locate the origins of the form? The groundwork was laid in the early years of Ancient Rome, at the temple of the Janus Gemini, where a two-headed god was placed over the ceremonial gates. In recent years, poor Janus has been bandied about by art critics with classical affectations, called upon as a fail-safe metaphor for intellectualising equivocation. A sculpture that looks different depending on the angle you view it from? A painting that depicts a threshold? Come hither, bygone two-beards! But although he was worshipped as the god of transitions, comings and goings, births and deaths, past and future, Janus was no mere poster-boy for poetical philosophising on the subject of liminality. In the ancient city of Rome, the gates of the Janus Gemini played a resoundingly symbolic function – flung open when Rome was at war, and closed only during peacetime. The latter would prove a rare occurrence. Following the death of the second king of Rome, Numa Pompilius, the temple doors are said to have remained open for a full four hundred years. When the empire officially converted to Christianity over a thousand years later, they had closed on no more than ten occasions.

As the civilised pursuits developed among wealthy Romans, as libraries were built and schools opened and little togad citizens gave recitals in the columned squares, the empire expanded its territory and coffers alike, with displays of remarkable brutality. All the while Janus watched on, one face looking out to the wars which saw Rome murder and enslave its way to global dominance, the other looking back at a culture blooming with advancements in gentility. Janus was unique in the pantheon as a Roman original, for unlike the majority of idols, he wasn't pillaged from the Greeks. Two distinct personalities attached to the same body, he was a god made in the image of Rome itself: a butcher and an aesthete.

Today, the Janus technique is popular among those for whom the promotion of selective civility is a useful distraction from all manner of heinous doings. 'The march today in Jerusalem isn't only a march of the LGBT community', said the Israeli Prime Minister Benyamin Netanyahu, channeling the god of old in a Facebook post prior to Jerusalem's 2016 Pride march, attempting a public burnishing of his humanitarian credentials. 'The participants in the gay pride parade will march for one principle: all human beings are equal, all human beings were created in the image of God, all human beings, male and female, have the right to live their lives along their own path with dignity and safety.' (Except, of course, if you are Palestinian.) Charles Saatchi also proved himself an advanced practitioner, when he staged the exhibition *Inside Pussy Riot*, an immersive account of the feminist Russian collective's experiences of being sent to jail, at his vast Chelsea mausoleum in 2017, thus assuming the unlikely mantle of champion of women who stand up to violent patriarchs. (The same Charles Saatchi photographed three years earlier strangling his then-wife Nigella Lawson over lunch at Scott's in Mayfair.)

In AD 363 the Emperor Julian was stabbed in the liver by a Christian soldier in his own ranks, and when he died from the injury, so too did the multi-god era of Roman paganism. In its wake a strange literature took hold, one of abject masochism, the holy poor, and the divinely under-sexed (whose followers, the turners-of-both-cheeks and givers-of-shirts-as-well-as-coats, displayed a surprising aptitude for wanton acts of shanking). And so it was that the spirit of double-tracking, only yet half-formed, departed the gates of the Janus Gemini, and watched on as armies of children were marched to their deaths, as the ink dried on the papal bull that lit the fires beneath half a million women, as the foreskins of the random dead were cut from bodies and sold as holy relics, all in the name of grace and innocence.

While Janus may have embodied the two-headedness essential to the double-tracking state of mind, and the middle-ages a deeply duplicitous piety, both were too explicitly nefarious to be counted as a fully-fledged manifestation. For though born of double standards, double-tracking is a phenomenon far more at home with a species of irony that remains, by and large, concealed from the subject upon which it operates, thus enabling its host to exist in a state of blissful cluelessness. (Until, that is, it's too late.) It would take more than two millennia from the building of the Janus Gemini gates before the art of looking considerably poorer than you are would arrive upon the world's stage fully formed, with a wardrobe, and prodigiously miscalculated political outlook, to match. And so to a spring morning in 1770, to the scene of the little Archduchess of the house of Habsburg Lorraine, daughter of the Austrian Emperor, and undisputed queen of double-tracking, exiting her carriage, on a bridge, on an island, in the middle of the Rhine.

The cleaner's press was in my jeans
And any eye for detail
Caught a little lace along the seams
Joni Mitchell

MADAME DEFICIT AND MIXED FORTUNES COUTURE

Maria Antonia (or Marie Antoinette, as she would soon be known) had arrived on the island to confirm her engagement to the French heir apparent. In order to ensure that the union proceeded with neither Austrian nor French noses out of joint – in the eighteenth century a misplaced curtsey was enough to trigger a diplomatic crisis – the girl's arrival was planned with an exquisite attention to choreography. When her carriage drew up on the bridge, the front wheels were placed on French soil, the back wheels in Savoy, and the doors situated in such a manner that the Archduchess would disembark in neutral territory. At only fourteen years old, she had already learnt to master the technique of the bifurcated identity. When her husband Louis XVI ascended the throne in 1774, he gave Marie Antoinette the Petit Trianon, a chateaux and grounds at the palace of Versailles. His father had built the chateaux for Madame de Pompadour, a woman groomed from childhood for a career as a royal mistress, after a fortune teller informed her mother that one day the little girl would rule the heart of a king. Madame de Pompadour died before work on the property was complete, and the chateaux became the home of her successor Madame du Barry, a former prostitute who successfully climbed the greasy pole of royal favour – much to the chagrin of courtly morals, Marie Antoinette's included. Once ensconced upon the throne, Louis XVI engaged in a flawless example of royal shade. To please his queen, he sentenced du Barry to holy labour by enrolling her at a nearby convent, thus banishing her in the guise of a blessing.

By the standards of Versailles the gift of the Petit Trianon from king to queen was positively decorous. What was unorthodox was the manner in which Marie Antoinette put the chateaux to use. In the monarchical system of the *Ancien Régime*, it was the right of every French citizen to visit Versailles and behold their rulers. In practice, this meant that the royals were treated much like treasures in a national museum – priceless articles flaunted to the masses with the aim of inciting pride and wonderment. Privacy was not part of the deal. The queen was followed around by courtiers, whose standing depended upon whether or not they'd earned such privileges as passing the young woman her knickers, and she was expected to eat her meals and even give birth before the public, who were more or less allowed to roam freely around the palace. 'It was impossible to move about the chamber, which was filled with so motley a crowd that one might have fancied himself in some place of public amusement', the royal chambermaid Madame Campan recalled of the night Marie Antoinette went into labour. 'Two chimney-sweeps climbed upon the furniture for a better sight of the Queen.'

Perhaps unsurprisingly, Marie Antoinette had different ideas when it came to affairs at the Petit Trianon. Breaking from royal convention, she employed the architect Richard Mique to create a private retreat on the chateaux's grounds, inaccessible to uninvited courtiers and unwanted public spectators. (This relative seclusion caused such a stir that for years it proved a rich source of rumour. One pamphlet, *The Royal Dildo*, contended that she used the secretive location to indulge in the 'German Vice', opting to wear loose clothing so that her female lovers could gain easier access to her 'sexual antechambers'.) Although clearly averse to seeing commoners while eating her supper, the queen did not want rid of them altogether. Or, more precisely put, she didn't want rid of the idea of them. Her plans for revamping the Petit Trianon included what stands today as the Valhalla of double-tracking, and the paragon of labour chic: the Hameau de la Reine, a model village on the chateaux's grounds, which contained a newly planted virgin wood, uprooted from the palace nursery, an entirely ornamental windmill, a barn, and a clutch of thatched buildings, complete with Flemish gables and a herb garden, in which the queen of France, a woman who thought nothing of wearing the 141 carat Regent Diamond pinned to her hat, wiled away her hours dressed as a milkmaid.

When it came to the inspiration for the hamlet, Marie Antoinette had a most unlikely guru: the political philosopher and staunch critic of private property Jean Jacques Rousseau, a man whose writings would inspire the revolutionaries who eventually beheaded her. Rousseau fever had taken hold in the homes of the wealthy following the publication of his novel *Julie, or the new Heloisie*, in 1761 – a romance of rustic values, and a book so popular that when demand outstripped supply, copies were rented by the hour on the streets of Paris. Enraptured by the sentimental aesthetic, the aristocracy paid little heed to the implications of Rousseau's politics, and an ill-fated fashion took hold for dressing as members of The Third Estate. When it came to fashion, of course, the queen was not a woman to be left behind. Such was the extent of her improvidence in this regard, that among the populace she acquired the nickname Madame Deficit. Her demands for new colours of silk could halt production for the entire industry, as was the case with *caca dauphin*, a brown silk introduced after the birth of her son, inspired by the hue of his shit-stained swaddling. She took a bellows to peasant chic, and when the Hameau de la Reine was complete, Rose Bertin, Marie Antoinette's designer, and a woman who amassed a vast fortune catering to royal fancies, dressed the queen accordingly. Among the staples of the new wardrobe were the Bonnet a la Rousseau, a great floppy affair adorned with ribbons and fresh flowers designed to look like a farm-girl's hat, and the gaulle, a loose linen top which shocked traditionalists for the manner in which it resembled peasant's underwear, and was worn, *zut alors*, unboned. A painting by Élisabeth Vigée Le Brun of the queen wearing the offending article caused such an uproar when it was displayed at the Paris Salon in 1783 that it had to be removed from exhibition, replaced by a near identical composition of the world's-most-high-born-commoner, this time bedecked in regal silks.

As Madame Deficit immersed herself in a fantasy of rusticania, famine set in among the peasantry. An uprising swept the kingdom known to posterity as The Flour Wars, which signalled the coming insurrection. The grain stores were empty due to chronic sovereign mismanagement, and in the space of three months over a hundred riots took place. Bakeries were ransacked, and those who attempted to profit from their neighbour's desperation were coerced into giving up their stock. 'The extreme inequality of our ways of life,' wrote Jean Jacques Rosseau, namesake of royal bonnets and beloved of Jacobins, 'the excess of idleness among some and the excess of toil among others, the ease of stimulating and gratifying our appetites and our senses, the over-elaborate foods of the rich, which inflame and overwhelm them with indigestion', were each the effects of a fallen people, which could have been avoided, he argued, 'if only we had adhered to the simple, unchanging and solitary way of life that nature ordained for us'. Headwear and horticulture, alas, only added to the tapestry of inequality into which Marie Antoinette's fate was woven.

In recent years Marie Antoinette's luxury peasant village, the Hameau de la Reine, has fallen into disrepair, populated only by a couple of pigs, a lonely donkey and a herd of luxury bunnies. But the orchestra can return the violins to their cases, for a saviour is in our midst, and it comes in the form of Dior – a fashion house ready to doff its hat to ancestry by funding a full renovation. Two and a quarter centuries after the heads of the king, the queen, the architect Mique and the exiled Madame du Barry all rolled off the stage at the Place de la Revolution, food for an infant republic nursed on blue blood, John Galliano unveiled his collection for Dior at Paris Fashion week, re-acquainting haute couture with the charms of poverty. Galliano took his direction from the French capital's homeless, and the outfits on display included silks printed to look like old, crumpled newspapers, pre-ruined cuffs and collars, and a few empty miniature whiskey bottles strung up as necklaces for good measure. 'One can't go into a restaurant without hearing fantastic young ladies talking about the fraying of tulle of the Christian Dior show', he reflected on the collection's reception. 'I didn't set out to make a political statement. I am a dressmaker. But jogging around the Seine has thrown Paris into a whole different light for me. I call it the Wet World. There are shades of Tennessee Williams and Marlon Brando. Some of these people are like impresarios, their coats worn over their shoulders and their hats worn at a certain angle. It's fantastic.' In 2008, he went further yet, unveiling a collection inspired by torture at Abu Ghraib, sending men down the runway covered in fake blood and body wounds, with hoods over their heads, ropes around their necks, and… Galliano-branded underwear.

Who could fail to cluck at such brazen displays of insensitivity? Haute couture, however, has never been a destination for those in search of prudence. 'It is better to be beautiful than to be good', said Oscar Wilde, recognising that fashion does not answer to the authority of morality. And, if there is something to be said for the upper echelons of the industry, it is surely its total transparency – an ability to anaesthetise all manner of histories and politics, botox out the wrinkles, and sell them back as covetable products. In this regard, Galliano is certainly not remarkable. Karl Largerfeld's mock feminist protest for Chanel is worthy of a mention, for which he sent a crowd of female models down the runway holding placards bearing such pressing demands as 'Fashion Not War' and 'Free Freedom'. (The same Karl Lagerfeld who helpfully offered the following advice for young women: 'If you don't want your pants pulled about, don't become a model! Join a nunnery, there'll always be a place for you in the convent.') Vivian Westwood had her models pushing supermarket trolleys full of junk, and let us not forget Jeremy Scott's collaboration with Adidas, in which a pair of high-top trainers with shackles attached managed to make it all the way from the drawing board to the factory floor, before eventually being pulled. 'You have nothing to lose but your chains', Karl Marx wrote in *The Communist Manifesto*, but perhaps even he could not have envisioned the extent to which the chains themselves would be commodified.

Like strange children tethered to the strings of giant birthday balloons, the very rich have a habit of drifting to alien altitudes, where oxygen is rare and self-awareness more so. Up here, residents pass the time wearing garments fashioned from cashmere clouds and tulle sunbeams, inspired by the citizens of distant Earth, whose effects are assumed and discarded as so many costumes in a planet-sized fancy dress box. Among these thoroughbred beneficiaries of capitalist inequity, only a gossamer interest in the origins of an aesthetic is entertained. One week's noose is the next week's silk kimono. Among the middle-classes, however, exists an infinitely more committed relationship with toil, and a delusion on an epidemic scale: the belief that a person has been born into the wrong class, and has been shunted up the ladder against their will.

And so in the autumn of 2017, I travelled to Marylebone, to the flagship store of Margaret Howell, in order to witness the class dysphoria of the bourgeoisie at close quarters. Howell's clothes adorn the employees of architect's ateliers, galleries, university faculties and publishing houses up and down the country, and she was once described by the *Financial Times* as the 'British designer most linked with haute workwear'.

Stepping on to the premises of a fashion store is rather like stepping into a showroom for a sect. At Margaret Howell, a complete lifestyle is mapped out and thematised, from homeware to clothing. Example believers are on hand, too, ushering customers in to the world of the upside-down, where people don't change out of their workwear when they want to look their best, but put it on instead. Howell's sect are the Amish of the Barbican: a group of affluent, cultured shoppers with a zealot's attachment to the manual labourer of yesteryear, among whom the 'Overall Dress', waxed hide 'Welders Jackets', and cow hide 'Coalman's Jerkins' are the vestments of the faith, and who appear to have dispatched of the past seventy-odd years in the same dustbin the Creationists dumped the dinosaurs. In person, Howell herself has the presence of a dunnock – discreet, fine featured, with a tan complexion acquired from repeat exposure to the English weather. 'I remember going to France on holiday and choosing one of those blue workwear jackets that the framers wear and loving that', she says, sitting across from me surrounded by rails of pea coats and sailor shirts. Does she have any interest in the equipment of today's labourer? 'I wear one of those high-viz vests for cycling', she offers by way of conciliation, before disappearing behind the thicket of a mug of own-brand Margaret Howell tea. 'I love wooden boxes, even a good cardboard box I like. But the plastic ones don't appeal so much. It's funny isn't it?'

Funny indeed. Up and up rises the detritus of yesterday's working-class, until the junk of an old market is a £40 vegetable crate on sale at an inner-city vintage fete. Such is the popularity of Olden Times that entire areas of London have been designated by property developers as sites of historical re-enactment. In the south-east of the city, where I am resident, the centre of Camberwell and nearby Bellenden Road (after a Dickensian fashion, the clue is in the name) have been renamed Camberwell and Bellenden Villages respectively. On these high-streets-turned-rustic-settlements can be found a Victorian green grocer, a 'purveyor of excellent artisan breads' – all 'made the old-fashioned way' – and a butcher's shop that specialises in 'heritage breeds', outside of which, in lieu of a sign, an ancient bicycle with a wicker basket is propped against the window. A dream of Albion, right in the heart of the city! A return to a time when high-street shops were the reserve of bearded white men in cotton aprons, who whistle as they work, mend their own bicycles, craft their own beer and cleave their own meat (and women could not vote, the destitute were sent to workhouses, and the economy was dependent upon the spoils of empire)! A vision of a true community, available to all (who can afford it)! The perfect place to wear a luxury denim 'Worker Jacket' (a steal at £345).

How to understand today's virulent strain of historical labour fetishation? After Madame Deficit's head departed her shoulders, the spirit of the double-tracker fled the scene. And well it might – revolutionary France was no place for the conspicuous calling-card of an elite who had taken to dressing in the garb of the same underclass whom they also systemically subordinated. When eventually it resurfaced, it did so as a love affair in Victorian Britain, taking root among the middle-classes, and at last finding its spiritual home. And so to a lawyer named Arthur Munby, and a maid of all service named Hannah Cullwick…

Arthur Munby was a barrister and a Cambridge graduate, who stepped into his father's profession with neither enthusiasm nor notable talent. Professionally unremarkable he may well have been, but away from work he was a singular figure. Munby referred to himself as 'a connoisseur of working-class women'. He spent his free time travelling across the UK in search of female labourers, making sketches and recording conversations of 'specimens' as he went, either photographing women at their place of work, or inviting them to attend a photographer's studio to sit for the camera under his direction. He also collected palm prints filthy from labour, which he acquired during his field-trips like a boy who takes rubbings from drain covers. So frequent were his walks through the poorer neighbourhoods of Victorian London that he was suspected of being Jack the Ripper, a murderer widely believed to be a gentleman with a predilection for working women.

'His ink was mostly spent on his life's hobby: big, strong and dirty women', wrote the historian Dianne Atkinson. Throughout his travels Munby kept extensive field notes, in which he recorded the customs and clothing of his subjects. Such was the case during a summer excursion he made to Lancashire, to view the 'pit brow lasses', women who separated coal from stone at the mouth of mine shafts. 'A hooded bonnet of padded cotton, pink, black or blue striped shirt open at the breasts, a waistcoat of cloth, generally double-breasted but ragged throughout, fustian or corduroy or sometimes black cloth trousers, patched with all possible materials except the original one', he noted down, with an attention to the sartorial details of poverty that would no doubt bring a smile to the lips of Rose Bertin, John Galliano, and Margaret Howell. 'Round the waist is tucked a petticoat of striped cotton, blue and black, rolled up as a joiner rolls his apron; it is never let down, and perfectly useless, only retained as a symbol of sex.'

One day in 1854, Munby spied an ideal 'specimen' crossing Oxford Street – a broad-shouldered young woman by the name of Hannah Cullwick, who was working at the time as a maid-of-all-service, one of the lowest and most demanding positions among a household's staff. The pair began a secret relationship that continued for over thirty years, and which, according to their extensive diaries and letters, was never physically consummated. Their relationship may not have entailed sex qua intercourse, but it certainly centred around a fixation on the power dynamic between master and servant, expressed via an embrace of dirt. Where possible, Cullwick would take on the grubbiest chores early in the day, so that she could appear at the front of the house to clean the steps 'in her filth', in the hope that Munby might arrive to watch her surreptitiously from across the street. He often did. If she was granted leave from the houses in which she worked, or was able to sneak out without attracting the attention of her employer, she would visit Munby at his rooms at The Temple, where it was not uncommon for her to lick the dirt clean from his boots, wash his feet, and if the mood took them, pick him up and carry him around the room like a giant gentleman baby.

Munby encouraged Cullwick to spend what little free time she had keeping a diary and writing him letters, in which she detailed the grubbiest aspects of her chores. For the pleasure of their relationship, she began to perform tasks beyond her job description that would cause her to become particularly soiled, such as scrubbing the inside of the chimney. 'Swept the passage and took the things out of the hole under the stairs Mary uses for dustpans and brushes', she wrote to him in 1878. 'It's a dark hole and about two yards long and very low. I crawled on my hands and knees and lay curled up in the dirt for a minute or so and then I got the hard brush and swept the walls down. The cobwebs and dust fell over me and I had to poke my nose out of the door like a dog's out of a kennel. Then I swept the floor of it and got my pail and cleaned it out and put the things back in their place.'

Eventually they married, but despite the vows, the union of a gentleman and a domestic would have caused a scandal, and so Cullwick moved into Munby's home at The Temple in the guise of a maid, sleeping in the servants' quarter in order to deflect suspicion. Their marriage may have remained unknown today if it wasn't for the letters and diaries – and Munby's liking for photographing Cullwick dressed in various costumes of hard labour. In a photograph of 1860, 'Hannah scrubbing the floor', she lies prostrate on the ground with a cleaning rag stretched out before her and a bucket by her elbow. 'Chimney Sweep', made two years later, shows a semi-naked Cullwick sitting cross-legged on the ground, her hair covered by a rag, her face and body smeared with grime, and her eyes turned obediently upwards, in a theatrical display of subservience. Visible around her neck is the 'slave collar' Munby gave to her – a thick choker, fastened with a lock to which only he had the key – which she wore around her neck for over twenty years. Munby carried a copy of this photograph of Cullwick in a locket, hidden, according to Atkinson, 'behind a photograph of her dressed as a lady'.

Like any good double-tracker, Munby considered his actions benevolently motivated, and his analysis of Cullwick's lowliness comes with a distinctly Beatitudinal ring. 'She has overcome the vanities and weakness of woman's nature and learnt to choose and absolutely delight in the vilest lot', he noted in his journal, preaching from the Sermon on the Slop Bucket. Blessed are the poor, for theirs is the kingdom of heaven; Blessed are the meek, for they shall inherit the earth; Blessed are the women servants, for they cook my meals and lick my boots.

Hannah Cullwick died in 1909, and Munby soon followed her under the soil. Over the coming century the middle-class continued to expand apace, its ranks bloated by the rise of bank clerks and copyists and administrators, and the many others who plied their trade in middle-management and bureaucracy. As it did, something extraordinary occurred. Rich and poor alike were sucked into the centre ground, creating, at its median, a cohort of educated and financially secure citizens, afflicted by a chronic sense of confusion. Do I suck upon a silver spoon or eat from a microwavable container? Wear loafers or Reebok Classics? Barber jacket or bomber jacket? Track suit or morning suit? Country estate or housing estate? Richmal Crompton or Straight Outta Compton? For where once Hannah Cullwick and Arthur Munby were two separate human beings, each in possession of a distinct body and biography, members of the new middle-class began to associate themselves with the role of both master *and* servant, two oppositional identities swirled into a single soul. Thus Arthur Munby and Hannah Cullwick conjoined to form the Munby-Cullwicks, a double-barrelled species, straight outta Crompton, just as committed to the finer things in life, as they are to the fetishisation of their imaginary working-class credentials.

For a garden-variety double-tracker, we need look no further than the urban home, and a subject that can tell us more about societal self-image than almost any other: dog ownership. In the city there exist a number of types of dog owner. The 'fuck-off look at me', who sets great store in being dragged around on the end of a chain by a large-jawed animal; the 'he's very friendly really', whose choice of violent pet betrays a masochism of a pre-meditated kind; and the 'beast of burden', who holds tight to a conviction that somewhere deep inside, somewhere fundamental, they are in fact a farm hand.

My mother, a long-term resident of the borough of Hackney, counts firmly among this latter category. She has a pet whippet named Tip, and like most of the other dogs who have lived on the street in recent years – the neurotic Manchester Terrier dosed up to the eyeballs on Prozac, the fat and balding Staff, the Chinese Powder Puff who lives at the house with the lilac door, and the little brown mongrel with a liking for golden showers – Tip spends his days lolling about on sofas and trotting around the park, transporting his collection of soft toys and doggy chews to and from various fleecy beds. Many are the occasion when I have heard neighbours discussing the practical nature of their pets – so much so, that if one had never visited Hackney, one may very well be forgiven for imagining that it's overrun by ratters, rabbit-catchers, bull-baiters and livestock herders. One afternoon, while standing in the kitchen with my mother, I happen to raise a Hula Hoop above Tip's snout. 'You can't feed him that', she says. 'Why not?' I reply. After all, whippets are not exactly an animal that require excessive attention to weight-watching. 'He's gluten intolerant.' Like the many hapless children of the borough, designated Gifted and Talented at the behest of over-eager parents who have fallen prey to the common mistake of confusing class for intelligence, Tip is an animal upon whom a variety of special statuses have been bestowed. As such, news of his dietary requirements came as no particular surprise. I look down at Tip, lying in his basket with his slender legs and sugar-white paws extended before him like the feet of a Louis XVI table. I look at his coat, a colour I have heard my mother describe on a number of occasions as champagne (notably when the dog himself is not present), and a colour which registers to all but the most discerning eye as beige. I look at the red dickie-bow fastened around his neck that my aunt gave him as a gift the previous Christmas. 'This is what we feed him now', my mother tells me, opening the fridge, and pulling out what I had previously mistaken for a luxury ready meal. But I stand corrected. For written on the cardboard sleeve, wrapped around a container filled with duck, butternut squash, spinach, sea kelp and Scottish salmon oil, are the words 'Working Dog'.

II
CASE STUDIES

A man is his own easiest dupe, for what he wishes to be true he generally believes to be true.
Demosthenes

TOBACCO AND CEDAR

A case study in interior design

'Here's to Guy, and the brilliant job he's done on the place. Mate really, I don't know where you found out about half of this stuff but it's *fucking fantastic.*'

Guy smiled modestly in acknowledgement and surveyed the warehouse. Nine months it had taken to transform it from a storage facility for knock-off handbags, and into a home for his cousin Millie and her husband Seb. And Seb was right. It did look good. The polished concrete floors, the exposed brickwork. Bricks, which had been shipped from Guy's grandmother's summer house in Brittany – it had taken all his know-how in the family diplomacy department to convince Nanou into knocking down that old atelier – and which, on arrival in Bermondsey, had been grafted on to the existing breeze-block walls.

'My favourite thing down here,' said Seb, 'has to be those lights. They're completely brutal!' The two pendant lampshades hanging from the ceiling really were something. A pair of wide, steel domes, their metal surfaces grazed with rust the colour of dried blood. Guy had bought them from a clearance sale at an old abattoir in Austria – mid-century classics he'd been assured – but the seller had been hazy on the specifics. Suspended now over the rugged, wooden table, they illuminated the party that had gathered for dinner: Seb and Millie, Guy, and Will, an old schoolfriend of Guy's who ran Seed, a photography gallery under the nearby railway arches, and who had sourced the large photograph leaning now against the atelier-brick wall.

'Tonight is a very special night, and we're so glad you could both be here. Not only is the warehouse officially converted,' Millie said, raising her glass and eliciting a small cheer in the process, 'but it's also Seb's fortieth this weekend. As a treat, Guy and I have kept one room in the house top secret. The en suite loo on the mezzanine has been completely out of bounds to poor Seb for a month now, and I know he's dying to see what we've got in there. But Guy made him promise, Scout's honour, that he wouldn't so much as peek.'

'And I've kept my word, haven't I Mills? But I must say, I haven't a clue what's up there.'

'You'd never believe me if I told you,' she replied, wrapping her arms around her husband's neck. 'But trust me, Guy's always been ahead of the curve. I'm going to embarrass him now, but I remember when he was a little boy and we were sailing on the *Octavia*... now, where were we Guy? That holiday when uncle Charlie had his moustache shaved off by that terribly severe local barber, when all he'd wanted was a trim.' Guy remembered it well, one of many Caribbean summers spent on Nanou's yacht. 'Yes, that's it, Turks and Caicos. Anyway, even though we were on the water almost the entire time – and when we weren't we were knee deep in sand or at the sailing club, and everyone knows how strict those old blazers can be – Guy insisted on bringing his skateboard *and* his turntable.'

Guy had changed in the fifteen years since that holiday, but not much. His eyes were still a bright, wet blue, only encased now behind tortoiseshell glasses. His cheeks were hollow where once they had been cherubic, but they retained the blush of the English orchard. His hair was a darker shade of sandy blonde – less Caribbean, more North Sea – and though he no longer skateboarded he applied the same distinction of care to his hand-built, bottle-green racing bicycle. Indeed, in recent months he had developed a fondness for keeping his bicycle clip around his ankle at all times – a sign of his indefatigable readiness, which also lit up terrifically well under UV. Although Guy did not like to boast, he had it on good authority that when he flashed his leg out from behind the DJ booth, the sight of that clip tight against denim could drive a woman wild.

The door to the kitchen opened, and two young women dressed in black entered the room. They placed before each person an oak board, on top of which was a mound of pulled pork, some pickles and three miniature brioche buns artfully stacked in a pyramid. As the food was being served, Millie cast an appreciative eye around the room. Everyone had been so generous. The photograph Will had installed that afternoon – at over six foot tall and framed in raw steel, it had taken four men to place it in position – was the perfect accompaniment to the meat-hook coatrack by the front door. She looked at Guy's canvas workwear jacket, hanging from it now. That labourer look had since come into fashion, and even Seb had a camouflage number knocking around in the wardrobe somewhere. But Guy had picked his up at a thrift store in San Francisco. An original, 1970s street-sweeper's jacket, municipal issue. An eye for authenticity, she thought, that was just so typical of him.

'When we started bouncing around ideas for this place, Guy said to me, "don't you think design should be naked?"', Seb said to Will across the table, who sagely nodded his agreement. 'And he was spot on. When you think about it, this country is going to the dogs – seriously, I read an article on it somewhere – the whole world is going to the dogs, because everyone has forgotten what it means to be human. I mean literally, how many people do you know who could actually hunt an animal and eat it? I'm talking about naked, red-blooded humanity.'

'Seb darling, where did you read that?' Millie chipped in.

'Oh, it must have been in *Lorgnette*, or *Nu-Gent* – one of those magazines. Anyway, what the guy said was, utility is more than just fashion. It's what we eat, what we wear, where we live. It's a whole *lifestyle*.' Seb broke off to punch at what remained of his pork, before sliding the beige meat into the last of his miniature buns. 'God this is delicious, Mills... So this guy got me thinking, when disaster strikes, and mark my word it will – when North Korea blows us to smithereens, or the polar bears land at Dover, and we all have to shoot birds from the pillboxes if we want to eat anything – who do you think are going to be the ones to survive? Not the magnolia walls brigade. They wouldn't last a single season. It'll be those who have learnt to appreciate utility. It'll be those of us who can hit a bird at sixty yards, train a dog to fetch it, and have a bloody great fire lit to roast the thing on. So with this place, we decided we wanted to get back to choosing things because we need them, get back to finding the beauty in use. What was that thing you said, Guy?' Seb asked, sucking the juice from his fingers. 'Yes, that's it – *make function the boss of form*. Guy showed us some converted warehouses where the wiring had been pulled out of the ceiling so you could see it, so the colour of the cables and the brick became the palette for the interior, and not Farrow & Ball or any of that mumsy rubbish. Millie fell in love with these aluminium air ducts we saw at this conversion off Clapham Common, didn't you Mills? It was an amazing place actually, the couple who owned it had installed a wood burning hot-tub on the decking, and all the furniture was made out of vintage vegetable crates. Anyway, even though we didn't have any air ducts here, Guy arranged to have one put in. Honestly Mills, you couldn't buy a better cousin.' They all looked up. A rainbow-coloured braid of electrical wires ran across the centre of the ceiling, to the left of which a metal air duct extended from one end of the room to the other, linking nothing to nowhere, but with a convincing affectation of purpose.

'Before we go upstairs to see the loo, Will,' said Millie, 'we've been desperate for you to enlighten us about that photograph.' Will turned towards the picture propped against the wall, and began to arrange his body in a manner that Guy had first seen at sixth form, and which invariably meant his friend was about to say something worth listening to. First, he separated his legs, so that his chinos pulled tight against his thighs. Then, as if he was simultaneously putting out two cigarettes, he slowly twisted the balls of both feet into the floor. Will's brow furrowed; the room bristled with anticipation.

'I wanted the photograph to be experienced right here with you, not like a window into a different world. I wanted to break down that fourth wall, so that the picture is *in this* room. That's why I decided to lean it, to show all of it, be true to the object.'

The photograph in question had been the product of a lengthy selection process. Seb had wanted a shibari print from Seed's last exhibition, but that had been ruled out as Nanou would be visiting in the spring, and she still suffered flashbacks from the time she got tangled in rope sailing *Octavia* solo off the coast of Dubrovnik (it had taken the lifeguard over an hour to unbind her). Guy had advised that it was probably for the best anyway, because as a rule of thumb, it's usually a good idea to buy artworks that you don't very much like. All truly profound works of art are ugly at first, and it is far better to learn to love something than to fall out of love too quickly. He had suggested instead they go for the photograph which stood framed before them now, a picture of a cardboard box on a gravel floor. The cardboard still bore the indentation of human buttocks where someone had evidently been sitting. A solitary weed grew out of the dirt, a cat – or perhaps a small dog, or else a severely dehydrated human – had relieved itself of two minute, lamp-black turds, and in the foreground an empty carton of cigarettes had been squashed into the gravel.

Will turned his attention once again to the task of grinding invisible cigarette butts. 'When you think about, this photograph is precisely about the essential beauty of the home. Even a cardboard box can be beautiful, and that crumbling wall is like a Rothko painting – its ambience, the way the colours fade in and out. It's like this guy, whoever the guy is that lives on this box, he's the lucky one.'

The reverie that spread throughout the room in the wake of Will's elucidations was broken only by the reappearance of the two women in black, who had come to clear the table. 'Ok', said Millie, 'I think Seb has waited long enough. Before pudding, will you do the honours and lead the way?' The group followed Guy, bicycle clip ablaze beneath the Austrian abattoir lighting, up the suspended staircase and on to the mezzanine. They passed Seb and Millie's bed, inset into the floor like a soft-furnished swimming pool, before coming to a halt in front of the toilet door. Guy snuck in for one final check, flicking on the light-switch in the process, and a few moments later that door, after a month of secrecy, swung-to.

The room inside was the size of a double bedroom, but it contained only two objects. A magenta neon light sprawled across the wide, back wall, like a drunken signature writ large upon the brickwork: illegible, but definitely profligate. Beneath the neon light, and bathed in its pink glow, was a stainless steel toilet. At the sight of it a hush bewitched the room – the sort of hard, sparkling quiet that follows a blow to the head. Seb and Will dropped down on their haunches like a pair of wicketkeepers. It was clear that this was no ordinary loo.

'It's like a pocket-knife', Seb said from his squatting position, his voice tuned tight by excitement. 'The way all the parts are combined in one.' And, after a fashion, he was right. Not only was the design remarkably compact, it had a potential violence about it too, that winked in the metal surfaces. The main bulk of the thing consisted of a broad, hexagonal column, fixed flush against the wall. Inset into the top of this column was a shallow sink, with a number of knobs populating the rim, and into its side, a circular recess, with space enough for a single roll of toilet paper. Right at its base, and practically kissing the polished concrete floor, was a broad, seatless steel bowl.

'Where on earth did you get it from?' asked Seb. 'Nasa?'

'Is it vintage Scandinavian?' Will offered, noting its minimal purity. 'I have a Danish 1950s dinner tray just like it, in steal and teak – it has a separate compartment for afters. Or perhaps it's something from the Donald Judd collection?'

'Even better', said Millie. 'Happy Birthday, darling – it's from an American prison! Guy says they have them all over the States, one per cell if the prisoners are lucky. That's why all the edges are rounded – so the prisoners can't prise the metal open and use the parts for weapons.'

'I bet', whispered Seb, who by now had lowered himself on to his knees, and was running his fingers over the cold, pink-tinged shaft in admiration.

Guy had first seen such a toilet installed at a friend's apartment in Manhattan earlier that year, and had known immediately that it was just the thing for Seb and Millie's conversion. His friend had bought his from a Stateside company that sells them chrome-plated, but Guy being Guy, he was convinced that the original steel model was much more honest. And so, throwing caution to the wind, he had decided to do some first-hand research, hitching a ride to San Quentin Prison with a fashion designer he knew, who was out there working on a new line of boiler suits. 'He scrapped the idea of vintage pretty quickly after that, let me tell you,' said Millie. 'He never got clearance to enter the prison, but the conditions were so awful in the local motel that poor Guy was bed bound and on a strict diet of Pepto-Bismol for an entire fortnight. In the end he had this toilet shipped directly from the manufacturer in China. There have of course been some upgrades,' she said, tugging at Seb's sleeve, and drawing him up to his feet. 'Press that button by the sink.'

Seb depressed a small, steel button, causing a fragrant gel to squirt out of a tiny hole and into the palm of his hand. 'Doesn't it smell good? Tobacco and cedar wood – Guy chose it especially.' Seb rubbed his hands together and inhaled deeply. 'Mate', he said excitedly, thrusting his fingers under Will's nose. 'I smell like I've been dragging hides across the Canadian wilderness!'

'But wait until I tell you the most amazing thing. Guy showed me: there are absolutely no joins, and no fastenings.'

It was true. Not a single piece of hardware could be seen upon its surface, and the metal was completely seamless, as if the entire thing had been welded from the inside.

'Did you notice how shallow the toilet bowl and the sink are? And there's nothing you can tie your boiler suit around either. It's completely suicide proof.'

It was the perfect object, each aspect of the form bossed by function, the apex of survival design.

THE PIOUS AND THE POMMERY

A case study of an art fair

I.

Where is the champagne? On second thoughts this is not entirely the right question. The champagne is in the ice trough, on top of the elegantly-worn Eames table behind the partition wall. The woman with a pom-pom on her head milling around beneath the late Frank Stellas has a glass of the stuff, as do the men in overcooked salmon slacks, the eternal palette du jour for collectors' trousers, but it doesn't seem likely that any of it is going to make it out of the booth they're standing in, at least not into my hand. Given the circumstances, *Who do I have to be to get a glass of champagne?* might well be the better question.

'Of course if it was up to us, and a lot of people we work with, you know, it would just be open to everyone the whole time,' Matthew Slotover, co-founder of Frieze Art Fair, had told me some weeks prior, a little unconvincingly. Because at 7 p.m. on 14 October 2015, standing in the aisle of London's most lucrative contemporary art fair on the opening night, the meticulously planned tiering system is as clear as the shoreline under the Saint-Tropez sun. Slotover has given me a 5 p.m. VIP pass, which in the Frieze running order makes me a fourth-class citizen. Above me are the VVIPs, who can access the tent from 2 p.m.; above them are the VVVIPs, free to mill around from midday; and above them are the VVVVIPs, persons of paramount importance who can enter the tent from 11 a.m., and are furnished upon arrival with a complimentary bag of beauty products. The 5 p.m. VIP pass, then, is for persons of distinctly ordinary importance.

But not to despair, because although I am only fourth on the ladder there are many more beneath me. There are the eager groups of art students sneaking in on the ticket of an art world friend, only to realise, once zapped through the guarded bag check, that Princess Eugenie is back in her castle, Benedict Cumberbatch has left the tent, and the champagne, that damn champagne, is anything but forthcoming. And then there are the eighty per cent of visitors to the fair who actually *pay* to get in, visitors who are also subjected to the rigours of tiering. *Be the first to see Frieze!* the website rather disingenuously advertises the Premium ticket, available at an extra cost on Wednesday when the fair first opens to the great and uninvited. By Saturday the collectors have cleared out their luggage from the cloakroom and departed the tent entirely, en route to Dubai or Moscow, having enjoyed the benefits of their non-domiciled status, a boon to the city's high-rolling international residents that makes splashing out at the fair particularly appealing. Or off to Paris's Grand Palais for the opening of FIAC, the next fair in the calendar, where many of the galleries at Frieze London will once again lay out their wares, before moving on to Cologne, Miami, New York, Hong Kong… or back across the park to the mansion houses of Primrose Hill for that matter, making way for the hoi polloi of London's culture-curious on Regent's Park's lawns.

If on Tuesday the fair is a chin-tuck in Dior brogues, by the weekend it's a schoolgirl with a Winsor & Newton sketchbook, diligently cross-hatching her way through a sculpture in the booth opposite, without noticing that seen from behind it is not, in fact, the sincere mid-century meditation on the union of landscape and female form she thinks it is, but a gigantic bronze penis, penetrating itself through its own Henry Moore-esque orifice; if only she had taken the time to walk around the thing, but she was put off by that rather stiff-looking Parisian gallerist in a tailored suit and trainer shoes, the one doing his utmost to appear as if he were alone with his MacBook in the 6th Arrondissement, waiting for a collector to arrive for a *vue intime*. Perspective, alas, is not something one learns from still-life lessons alone...

Art fairs have a habit of showing everyone present in an unsympathetic light. Because, of course, the gallerist is not there to offer free tours to school children but to sell art, and has stumped up a five-figure sum for a booth in a prime location, money that will not be repaid by acts of benevolent pedagogy. And that girl studying the bronze, has she not in fact arrived with the rather commendable notion that one might learn something from art, and was she not also enticed to the tent by Frieze itself, which publicises the fair as a place to buy art, yes, but also as a glittering pin thumbed into the map of the cultural landscape? 'Experience moments of immersion and interaction', says the press material, 'encounter impressive outdoor works', 'explore Frieze Projects, the fair's non-profit programme of artists' commissions'. *Experience, encounter, discover, explore...* words tailored to an altogether different audience than *buy, sell, network* and *speculate*.

Herein lies the crux of Frieze London. It is everything all at once, trade fair and cultural institution, commercial and non-profit, a fair that commissions artists at the same time that it is paid by galleries to show them. Frieze is a microcosm of the art world from the fringes to the moneyed core, and reveals all its dazzling paradoxes. These were paradoxes, I decided, that I should like to get to the bottom of. And so, in the run-up to the 2015 edition of Frieze London, I spoke to three people who have been involved in the fair from its inception – the former Young British Artist Jake Chapman, super-collector Candida Gertler, and the co-founder of Frieze Art Fair, Matthew Slotover – as well as a number of newcomers and casualties, in order to track the various beliefs and investments that follow artworks as they pass through the heart of the market.

II.

'When I go to Frieze I think a lot about the idea that if there was an overnight virus and everyone died, and the Martians came down and started trying to catalogue what the fuck people were up to, you know, there would be certain things they could say *yep, yep, absolutely, we get that.*' Jake Chapman breaks off from his story, one of many he would tell me over the course of an afternoon at his gated studio complex in Hackney Wick, and picks up the glass in front of him as an example. 'But there'd be certain things they'd be looking at saying *what the fuck is this?*' I ask whether the aliens would approve of the artworks he makes with his older brother and collaborator, Dinos. 'It wouldn't last. Ours wouldn't, no!' Would the aliens not understand, I enquire, the artworks they produced? 'I think they would understand them, they'd think children made them! Weird children, very disturbed children.'

Jake Chapman is a big man. His face is peppered with stubble, where his head is not bald it is shaved close to the skull, and his arms are covered in scrappy homemade tattoos. When we meet he is dressed in a camouflage t-shirt, jeans and heavy leather boots. But despite his imposing figure, there is something disarmingly innocent about him. His eyebrows point upwards in the middle in an expression of mild and pleasant surprise, he is prone to debilitating bouts of giggles, and while his rampant verbosity might be unbearable in someone else, even the most convoluted of tales are turned sweet on Chapman's lips, tales which he delivers with the freedom and gaiety of a bird singing in a tree. These qualities combine in him, so that whatever the argument he is busy extolling, whether Armageddon or the existential crisis of the artwork at an art fair, he gives the impression that his spirit, for all the world, is as light as candy floss. Here is a man able to be at once deadly serious and completely infantile, and who has built a career out of it.

'I remember Matthew Slotover and Tom Gidley coming up to me years and years and years ago, and they gave me a little piece of paper, a little photocopy', Chapman tells me, breaking into a very silly voice. 'And they came up and they said, *we're gonna do a…* they were really little, you know… *we're gonna do this magazine, it's gonna be called frieze, and we're wondering if you'd like to write for it.* And I remember thinking, ah, that's sweet. And look at it now.'

The Frieze empire began with *frieze* magazine – founded by Slotover, Amanda Sharp and artist Tom Gidley in 1991 – and rose to prominence with the Young British Artists – a group whose swaggering, shock-baiting antics featured heavily in the early editions, and who now command vast sums on the international market. The Chapman brothers are among those associated with the YBA moniker who went on to become household names, along with the galleries and dealers who made them. Jay Jopling, owner of White Cube gallery, continues to represent the Chapmans to their mutual benefit; he also launched the careers of Damien Hirst and Tracey Emin. Jopling was never a poor man – the son of a Conservative Baron, he was educated at Eton – but his estimated fortune of £100 million has certainly been bolstered by White Cube's commercial success. 'I always liked to collide the establishment with the avant-garde', he said of his *modus operandi* in an interview with the *Financial Times'* art critic Jackie Wullschlager. 'In art world terms,' Wullschlager explains, Jopling '*is* the establishment.'

Chapman tells me that he wrote for *frieze* magazine on a number of occasions, but stopped after deciding that it was too 'humane' and 'confessional'. One of Damien Hirst's now trademark butterfly pictures featured on the cover of the first edition – a staple-bound magazine with a flimsy, callow charm. By the time that the 174th edition came out in October 2015, the magazine had a print readership of 320,000, and three of the world's most prominent art fairs had opened under the Frieze umbrella: Frieze London, Frieze Masters, which joins the original fair on the lawns of Regent's Park, and Frieze New York.

Shortly before the opening of Frieze London 2015, I visit Matthew Slotover at Frieze HQ, on the top floor of a converted

Victorian poor school in Shoreditch. The door to his glass-walled office opens, and Slotover rises with a slow, broad smile. He looks good, a trim figure with dark, close-cropped hair who shows little evidence of approaching fifty. To the right of his desk is a lounge area of mid-century furniture in black leather and dark hardwood. A rubberised pannier bag unclipped from Slotover's bicycle is propped against the wall, and strapped to his wrist, catching the light as it cascades through the Victorian window panes, is the blank, glossy face of the latest Apple smart watch.

The initial idea for *frieze*, he says, was to 'promote young artists and sell their work directly through the magazine', but the plan changed when he was advised that wasn't how the industry worked, 'that you go through the galleries and there's a reason for that', and that it would be 'tacky' to sell art through a publication. A nascent contemporary art magazine, of course, would considerably hamper its chances of success by cutting out galleries, the same art world professionals who form an integral part of *frieze's* readership, and who shell out upwards of £3,000 for a full-page advertisement (advertisements which, in 2015's November edition, account for roughly half of the magazine's content). The initial idea to sell art through the magazine was not so much dropped as re-calibrated. Page space and not artworks would be the object in which *frieze* traded, allowing artists and galleries to become 'friends', as Slotover calls them, rather than direct competitors. 'Doing a magazine', he tells me, 'you get to know artists, you become sympathetic towards them. Of course you're supposed to be critical about them but generally you're on their side. And if something's not interesting, we just don't cover it.'

It would not be until 2003 that Frieze London first pitched its gargantuan white tent on Regent's Park's lawns, but the seeds for the magazine's expansion had been sown some years prior. In 1995, *frieze* published an article by photographer Collier Schorr titled 'Who is the Fairest of Them All'. 'The art fair,' Schorr opens, 'is the most frequented and beleaguered event manufactured by the art world.' Full of moustachioed dealers wearing braces and monk shoes, she suggested they were no place for the future faces of the market. There was, however, an exception – for Schorr, and significantly for the young Matthew Slotover – and it came in the form of UnFair.

UnFair was established in 1992 by a group of galleries who had been denied booths by a dinosaur of the fair circuit, the prestigious and long-running Art Cologne. Unlike Art Cologne, held in the great trade fair halls on the edge of the city, UnFair took place in a disused department store in the centre of town. The stuffy old world had been banished; this fair had renegade status.

Slotover recalls UnFair fondly. 'They had Motown playing over the tannoy,' he tells me, 'and Damien Hirst was at the tiny White Cube stand, and he put twins sitting on the stand next to twin frankfurters in formaldehyde – *because it was in Cologne*,' he says, grinning. It was at UnFair that the YBAs began to shine in the eyes of the international market; it was at UnFair that the market place could, at long last, be cool.

Gregor Muir, now the director of London's ICA gallery, remembers UnFair through similarly rebel-tinted spectacles. 'I hitched a ride to Cologne with *frieze* magazine', he writes in his memoir *Lucky Kunst: The Rise And Fall Of Young British Art*, with none other than a young Slotover behind the wheel. After an encounter with an artist pretending to be unpacked from a shipping crate, who 'delivered a thigh-slapping proclamation that he would continue to live in his crate for the duration of the fair', Muir headed to the opening party with Jake Chapman.

'The atmosphere was exhilarating', Muir continues, 'everyone dancing to the thumping beats that reverberated through the vast interior. I looked up from my triple vodka and tonic and saw Anthony Reynolds, an otherwise reserved London gallerist, boogying on the dance floor.' The night did not end there. At two in the morning, Muir and Chapman returned to the fair, arriving the picture of rebellion, 'utterly inebriated' and covered in crumbs 'from the collection of cakes we'd stuffed in our mouths after passing a bakery preparing for the day ahead'. Once inside, Muir helped himself to beer from behind the bar, and Chapman began swapping the paintings between booths – that is until Muir intervened, fearing their antics would provoke such grave retribution that the pair would be 'deported'.

UnFair ended after only two years, but it showed that at a fair one really could have it all – boogying gallerists, pickled wieners, performance artists and no end of minor rebellions. Best of all, like an anarchist fancy-dress party in a hedge-fund office, was the potential to have all this while making vast sums of money.

'We would go to the art fairs in Cologne', Slotover tells me, 'and Basel and Paris and Madrid, and think, "Wow, these are great". And we would go there as art critics to try and find out about the art, and meet the dealers, and see what artists were doing. So we always thought art fairs were great places, not thinking at all about the buying and selling of it, just as a way of communicating.' The first Frieze fair was unveiled in 2003, with 124 galleries from across the world participating. By the end of the week, £20 million of sales had taken place within the tent, with Frieze making just shy of £1 million from renting out floor space alone.

III.

The Chapman brothers have been frequent exhibitors at Frieze Art Fair since its inception, showing in the blue-chip section at the front of the tent. If access to the fair is subject to a strict tiering process, so too is the tent's topography, with galleries organised alphabetically into zones from front to back according to status. Up the ramp at the entrance, drop off your luggage, through security, locate your zone… Universal Studio, the firm who designed the tent, are masters in the art of transforming corporate non-space into a luxury destination. Also on their résumé: the Fortnum & Mason Champagne Bar at Heathrow's Terminal 5.

The bulk of exhibitors – commercially established galleries working with commercially established artists – are in the Main Stand, with the blue-chippers in the A zone by the entrance where the cost of floor space enters five figures. Such outlays can be recuperated in a single sale: at White Cube's stand in 2015, Damien Hirst's painting *Holbein (Artist's Watercolours)* (2015) sold for just under one million before lunchtime on the opening day.

At the back of the tent, bringing up the rear in zones G and H, is the Focus section for younger galleries. Here careers are less established, business more precarious, floor space is cheaper and there is pressure, particularly on debutante galleries, to show artworks of a less straightforwardly commercial nature. 'If you want to get in the club', artist Samara Scott tells me, having embedded a pond of fizzy drinks, shampoo and various perishable matter directly into the floor of the tent for the maiden voyage at Frieze of the gallery that represents her, South London's Sunday Painter, 'you have to do a difficult initiation act'. Once the hazing is over, a gallery can pull out the plinths, hang the paintings, and take the easier route to making sales. But 'it would be distasteful', Scott says, 'for a young, upcoming gallery to do something so… *oh my god! transparently commercial, how disgusting!*

One of the Chapmans' most memorable outings at Frieze London was *Painting for Pleasure and Profit* in 2006, for which they set up shop in White Cube's booth painting half-an-hour portraits for £4,500 a pop. 'I could see what Dinos was doing,' Chapman says of this venture, 'he could see what I was doing, but the people sitting couldn't see, so we'd do two people at the same time, and it was the funniest. He did the most beautiful, really beautiful, *exquisite* painting of this demure Spanish woman who sat down, paid her money – and it was not an insubstantial amount – and he painted her and she had this lovely necklace and beautiful silk dress, and he painted this. And then he painted this severed neck!' Chapman's face concertinas in giggles; evidently, he is immensely pleased by the memory of the decapitated subject. 'Just the idea of sitting down and *not* getting your portrait done!'

The demure Spanish woman in the silk dress would have been disappointed, of course, if the Chapmans hadn't come up with something suitably puckish. The pair thrive on playing the court jester, of presenting the apparently unpresentable to their audience. Among their biggest feats to date are buying a set of Francisco Goya's 'Disasters of War' etchings from the early nineteenth century and defacing them for an exhibition at White Cube in 1999, and adding rainbows and love hearts to watercolours painted by Adolf Hitler – at least ostensibly, the pair have form when it comes to the art world hoax – for their exhibition *If Hitler Had Been a Hippy How Happy We Would Be* at White Cube in 2008. Gruesome portraits to order, by their standards, are relatively tame fare. At 2007's fair they were back at White Cube offering to deface £20 and £50 notes for fairgoers, free of charge – an exhibit that Candida Gertler, art collector and founder of philanthropic organisation Outset, described as among her favourite exhibits to date.

I met Gertler at the Greenberry Café in Primrose Hill to find out more about the tightly entwined genesis of Outset and Frieze London, as well as the curious attraction of the super-rich to the 'non-profit' sides of the art world. With her ringed fingers sparkling in the north-west London sun, Gertler eased into an origin story of how she, Sharp and Slotover had concocted the plan while out for dinner one night 'in a little Korean restaurant' in 2002. The details of this story were evidently important, as if the smallness of the restaurant and the fact that it was Korean displayed not only the intimate relationship she had with Sharp and Slotover, but a subtler form of sophistication. When one could very well eat every meal at the Ritz, it is those things which not only have to be paid for but discovered that are the mark of the truly cultivated.

They hatched a plan: to create a fund of money – £150,000, made up of individual pledges from private donors in Gertler's network of friends and associates – with which artworks would be bought at Frieze London and donated directly to the national collection at Tate. One of the artworks on Outset's shopping list for 2004's fair,

Roman Ondák's *Good Feelings in Good Times* (2003), would become the first work of performance art ever owned by the Tate. Ondak's piece consisted of performers instructed to line up in queues between seven and fourteen strong, reading papers, twiddling their thumbs, in areas of the fair where one might not expect a queue to form.

Good Feelings in Good Times was exhibited as a part of the non-profit Frieze Projects, a section of the fair Gertler describes as showing '*less obviously commercially viable*' artworks. Unlike the majority of artists participating in the fair, whose work is displayed in booths paid for by the galleries that represent them, artists showing as part of Frieze Projects are commissioned by in-house curators to produce site-specific work. Dotted around the tent as a series of theatrical and participatory interludes, the Projects bring to the fair something missing from the rows of paintings and objects on plinths which – typically having little to no conceptual relationship with the tent, the artworks they are displayed alongside or the fair itself – appear ready to be packed up and shipped on. The Projects take seriously the fair's ambition to be a space of curatorial as well as financial value; they make Frieze appear less like a bazaar and more like an exhibition.

'There was no price tag to it', Gertler tells me, recounting the purchase of Ondak's work, 'I remember standing in the corridor with Jessica Morgan [then the Curator of Contemporary Art at Tate Modern] who was at the time part of our team, and Roman said "I don't have a price for it", and then they disappeared, and you know, there was two minutes of conversation, and they came back with "£8,000". OK! £8,000!'

Gertler's excitement at having bought an artwork without a price tag was palpable. But in reality, buying a performance work from the non-profit section of the fair is like asking a shopkeeper if you can buy the jacket on the mannequin in the window. It might not be the obvious choice, it might be, as Gertler so aptly put it, less obviously commercially viable, but it is a request that is hardly likely to be denied. A shop is a shop, a market is a market, a fair is a fair, and for the right price everything is for sale.

There is evidently an appeal in aligning oneself with artworks that have a less explicit relationship with commerce. Like that *little Korean restaurant*, such artworks offer something that the big names of the art market do not. When having the bank balance of a multi-millionaire is qualification enough to hang a 'Spot Painting' by Damien Hirst in the stateroom of your superyacht, buying the ostensibly un-buyable is an especially piquant pleasure. By this logic, it is perhaps unsurprising that when Gertler lists her favourite exhibits at Frieze to date, the list should include three exhibits that are *less obviously commercially viable*, and which all also involved waiting in line – an experience of thrilling mundanity, one can only assume, for those unacquainted with Lidl on a Sunday afternoon. In addition to Ondák's queue and the Chapman's defaced bank notes, topping Gertler's list is rolling down a grass slope as part of Paola Pivi's installation for the Projects section in 2003, a popular attraction that required a brief spell of the much enjoyed hanging around.

IV.

The Chapman brothers have been granted the keys to Frieze City, and in his studio, Jake Chapman runs me through a number of convoluted and improbable suggestions they have floated concerning their participation. 'We wanted to do a booth where you could go and buy someone else's work from somewhere else and bring it to us and we'd change it.' The flaw in this proposal, alas, was 'the unpredictability of people's egos'. Another idea involved offering 'free money' to homeless people at the fair. For this, he tells me, 'we'd need to have an ATM, we'd have us drawing, and what people would have to do is take out £20, give homeless people £10 and we'd draw'. But the mother of all proposals, also including the unsuspecting homeless, was one suggested to Miuccia Prada, head of the luxury goods dynasty, and a major patron of the arts.

'We had another idea to do a show in Milan at the Prada Foundation, and I just remember sitting and talking to Miuccia Prada and suggesting this as a possible idea. It was called *Tramps on Ice*. We wanted to build a big ice rink – because Milan is full of smackheads and a terrible sort of drug population, *sub*-population – and we'd say if you come there you'd get some money and a free dinner. But you have to ice skate for an hour. I mean it's hugely fascistic but the idea was that when they arrive, they skate for an hour, and then they have a shower, then when they come out we take their clothes, we put them on a hanger and put Prada labels in their clothes, they get Prada clothes, they get a meal and then they leave. So the show's on for three months, the clothes would get less and less worn because the same people would be coming and bringing back Prada clothes and getting fresh Prada clothes. We'd bottle the shower water and call it *Eau de Tramp*, and the by-product is that these drug addicts would end up being brilliant ice skaters. Win win! Obviously they didn't really go for that.'

There was, however, 'lots of laughing'. And that, of course, is precisely the point. Neither Frieze nor the Prada Foundation – a cultural organisation with a permanent exhibition space in Milan, in a building designed by Rem Koolhaas, one part of which is clad in 24-carat gold leaf – were going to entertain ideas that poke such extensive fun at the conspicuous wealth behind their operations. Not to mention allowing the homeless through their doors, which at Frieze would require extending the fair for at least another week, in order to make space for all the rungs on the social ladder between the VVVVIPs and the destitute – but both were no doubt pleased to be in on the merriment, just as the demure Spanish lady would have been pleased with her severed head. This is the particular appeal of the Chapman brothers. Not only do they have license to mock the cultural aristocracy, but the aristocracy actively enjoy it – it adds a little *frisson* to proceedings.

V.

The rebellious, anti-establishment posturing of the Chapman brothers is more come-on than call-out, a characteristic that has no doubt aided their continuing popularity. Art is a decidedly social industry, where business doubles-up as pleasure; an industry in which clients are friends. Accordingly, collectors don't just want the clay or the paint or pound shop dreck transformed into cultural gold, they often want a relationship with the alchemist too. And so, as much as artists ply their trade in the studio, they must also ply it on the social circuit, enabling the rich to journey vicariously to the exotic lands of the (relatively speaking) poor, without ever mentioning the arms or the oil or the property portfolios that bankroll such boutique vacations, or the promise of money that explains why the artist is present in the situation at all. 'I feel at times like a weird escort', Samara Scott told me shortly after the 2015 fair, smarting from the pressure of having to socialise with potential business interests. 'I mean you don't have to sleep with them, but there's an exchange that you have to give.'

Frieze London's own flair for presenting the allure of hardship to those who will never experience it reached its zenith at 2015's talks programme, organised by the Lucky Kunst himself, Gregor Muir. The talks covered a range of subjects from the social impact of museums to the imprisonment of art activists and the legacy of punk. But the stand-out event was a panel discussion, titled 'Off-Centre: Can Artists Still Afford to Live in London?'

The event was so popular that tickets had to be reserved in advance, and attendees were advised to arrive twenty minutes early. Behind me as I waited in line a young man in a fur hat and a brocaded coat so long that it tickled his ankles knocked back a midafternoon glass of champagne. By this point the entire queue ought to have known, in fact should have known already, why the talk we were yet to see was flawed. For there may be many artists struggling to afford the cost of London living, and many non-artists for that matter who cannot afford the rise in rent ushered in by the influx of artists, who set up studios in poorer areas of the city, shortly to be followed by coffee shops and craft breweries and property developers, but not one of those people was to be found among the fur hats and the £36 entrance tickets. Nevertheless, such a dose of political engagement makes for a bracing digestif, following those Serrano ham croquettes in the VIP lounge.

'The exemplary double-tracker', wrote Tom Wolfe in *The Painted Word* in 1975, arrives at a private view at MoMA in a dinner jacket and paint splattered Levis, exclaiming "I'm still a virgin! (Where's the champagne?)"' Yet within the arts, double-tracking is not only a pious mask to cover the whims of the wealthy. It is the thing that allows us all to appreciate the painting on the gallery wall without being deluged by the thought of the machinations and the millions that led to it hanging there. It is what enables us to engage with the world not in its unsavoury entirety, but as an artist presents it to us, and as we ourselves would like to see it. Without it, it is questionable whether there could be any art appreciation at all. What distinguishes double-tracking from its less discerning relatives – the flip-floppers and the U-turners and the outright conmen – is that it cannot be easily faked or fudged. For the gallery, for the artist, for the middle-men and for the viewer alike, double-tracking requires dedication, and most importantly of all, it requires *belief*.

As a sign of the significance of this faith, it must be upheld even in the most explicitly commercial contexts. It is something that Frieze insists be carried out throughout the fair, right down to the selection process. Following 2015's fair I spoke with Barnie Page, who was at the time a director of the London gallery Limoncello. Page told me he knew a number of figures on the London commercial scene who had applied repeatedly to get into Frieze London, but were routinely rejected. The reason, he told me, was that they were seen as 'dealers' and not 'gallerists'. While a gallerist is both a businessperson and a pious servant of the arts – a gallerist must be able to vouch for the quality, and not just the marketability, of the artworks they promote – to be branded a 'dealer' is to be tarnished by purely avaricious interests. It is to adhere, and fatally, to only a single track.

VI.

In 2010, Matthew Slotover took part in a debate at the Saatchi Gallery. The motion: 'Art Fairs Are About Money Not Art'. Slotover, in the 'no' camp along with artist Richard Wentworth and critic Norman Rosenthal, was pitched against Louisa Buck of *The Art Newspaper*, artist and writer Matthew Collings, and a then-painter named Jasper Joffe.

Joffe was present because he had set up The Free Art Fair, a short lived, alternative model of fair at which artworks were not sold but given away at the end via an elaborate raffle. 'For once', reads the now obsolete press material, 'instead of art going to the highest bidder or those who can afford it, someone who really loves an artwork will be able to have it for free.' The Free Art Fair had some limited success: of its three incarnations, one was held at the Barbican Centre, and it attracted a number of well-known artists, including Bob and Roberta Smith and Joffe's sister, the painter Chantal Joffe.

At the debate focus inevitably shifted to Frieze, and Joffe – the least known of the group and evidently the least proficient in the etiquette of debating – lost his cool. Anger tuned his voice, his ample curls were furiously smoothed against his skull, and his cheeks flushed crimson. His main gripes: Frieze exhibits more men than it does women, the selection process is run by a cartel of gallerists, and that by pandering to the tastes of the rich, Frieze does a disservice to the majority of underpaid artists.

Slotover responded coolly, adhering to rule number one of debating: that showing one's emotions is a mistake on par with a fox offering its bottom to the hounds to sniff. He began by pointing out the history of unequal representation at Joffe's own fair, listing the disproportionate number of male participants from The Free Art Fair's press material, before reminding the audience that eighty per cent of visitors to Frieze Art Fair come to spectate and not to buy. Hardly, he argued, a statistic befitting an avaricious cartel.

Later that same year an artwork of Joffe's was removed from Frieze London. London radio station Resonance FM had been invited to participate in Frieze Projects, and planned to use their booth to hold an auction as a fundraiser. One of the intended lots was a painting by Joffe of a po-faced Nicholas Serota, director of Tate, with the words 'Cheer Up Love' painted in the background amid a sea of polka dots. Frieze removed the painting before the auction began, citing the fair's 'strict policy of selection'. 'I presume,' said Joffe at the time to the *Independent* newspaper, doing his best to at least go down in flames, 'it is because I was recently in a debate at the Saatchi Gallery with Matthew Slotover, and he seemed quite upset and angry that I criticised Frieze.'

I mention to Slotover that I had seen this debate. Joffe, he tells me, had made a 'big deal' about their confrontation afterwards. He 'edited my Wikipedia page to make it really big, and stuff like that. It's all been a bit... *stalkery*.' And, as a final nail in poor Joffe's coffin, 'not being selected, I think, was his main problem'. This seems a rather cruel dispatching of the subject, cruel, because it was no doubt true. *If something's not interesting we just don't cover it*, Slotover said of the magazine's selection policy, and at the fair, as it is at the magazine, not being selected is a judgement that offers little room for reply.

'Facts,' wrote Aldous Huxley, 'do not cease to exist because they are ignored.' The same cannot be said for careers in the arts. A week prior to meeting Matthew Slotover, I had breakfast with Joffe. At his suggestion we met in a co-operative café in Hackney, the day before it was due to shut down. Over rye bread toast and fair-trade coffee Joffe spent an hour expounding on the evils of the art world, revealing that he has subsequently quit art altogether, setting up in publishing instead. The narrative of being a dangerous agitator excluded from the market, a Guevara to Slotover's Kennedy, disarmed of his aggravating spotty canvases, evidently suited him well – just as it suited Slotover to write Joffe off as 'stalkery'.

'I would question people who feel they're excluded from Frieze. Are they excluded from other fairs as well, that have nothing to do with us?' Slotover reasons, considering from the apex of the golden ladder the man who has slipped down a snake to the bottom of the board. 'Unfortunately, a lot of the time you come to the same conclusions. And not through any collusions because it's not in anyone's interest. So, you know, it's competitive. But life is competitive!'

VII.

Slotover's fondness for broadcasting that eighty per cent of Frieze Art Fair's visitors come as spectators and not buyers is a masterstroke of double-tracking, which does much to reframe the fair as something other than a trading floor. It is a statistic that can be found repeated in numerous publications. *The New York Times* have it, *The Spectator* too. It is even cited, no less, in the first lines of Frieze Art Fair's Wikipedia page. And come the non-buying spectatorship do, for there is nowhere better to see a comprehensive who's-who of the commercial art world. The fair provides an annual survey of the artists and artistic trends at the forefront of the international market. It also provides an opportunity to witness gallerists and collectors in action, those agents of the commercial art world so often invisible to the gallery-going public, and so often just out of reach for aspiring artists.

What was not listed on Frieze's Wikipedia page was the pleasure of arriving at the fair as one of the twenty per cent, with the sole purpose of spending large sums of money. And so at Frieze HQ, I ask Slotover perhaps the most obvious question of all. Why is buying an artwork better than simply looking at it? 'Well, like you I never used to own it, partly because I couldn't afford it – but you know there are editions and things that one can buy that are not expensive', he says, graciously empathising with my financial status, before taking the opportunity to advertise the cheaper end of the market. 'When you go to a fair it takes on a different atmosphere when it's like, "OK, I'm gonna buy something". There's an excitement about it, and you're looking at art with that view, so it's like, "OK, what do we like, how much is it, is it available?" And you kind of have a motive, you know, a mission. And then you buy it and the dealer's really happy and the artist's really happy, and then you get it shipped home or you take it home, and you find somewhere in your house for it, and you look at it every day. And then a year later you might move it around, brighten up a room that was a bit dull or boring before, and it's amazing.'

The dealer's happy, the artist's happy, the new owner's happy – the art fair, according to this description, is at least a peaceable kingdom.

The suckling child may well be playing on the hole of the asp, or have his hand in the cockatrice's den for that matter, but only, one suspects, because he has learnt to tolerate the poison. Slotover's vision of the fair is a far cry from that of British artist Jesse Wine, who first showed at Frieze Art Fair in 2013 with his London gallery Limoncello, and who entered the proceedings by way of a baptism of fire. In order to secure their place in the Focus section of the tent, dedicated to younger galleries, Limoncello proposed that the three young men they were exhibiting would be present in the booth alongside their work for the entire duration of the week.

It is highly unusual for an artist to man their own booth. After overseeing the installation of their work, if indeed their oversight is required, artists appear tentatively in the tent, at the private view, to meet with collectors or journalists at the request of their gallery, or to take a furtive, midweek glance at what else is on display. (A case in point. When I ask Jake Chapman if he will be participating in 2015's fair, he replies with the sort of nonchalance that is the sole preserve of the firmly established: 'I think Jay will probably drag something down there'.) Unless an artist is in a position of power so considerable that they are able to demand complete control over the manner in which their work enters into circulation, they keep their presence to a minimum and for good reason. 'Artists don't make art to make sales', Wine tells me, but at Frieze the boundary that distinguishes an artwork from a commodity, and an artist from an escort, is in serious danger of dissolving.

This, then, was a masterstroke for a young gallery: to say to the beast how beautiful it is, what a pleasure its company. Abercrombie & Fitch may employ the services of shirtless, six-packing gym bunnies to entice customers into their stores, but they've got nothing on the appeal of three fresh-faced colts at an art fair, instructed to be as available as possible and no doubt rendered desperate by the task at hand. For six days Wine stood in the booth, enticing the passing crowds to stop for a while, to take a seat with him on one of the chairs provided with such *tête-à-têtes* in mind. 'I just sort of thought,' he says of the experience, 'if I look the devil in the eye a little bit with this art fair stuff, and am present and see exactly how it works, and see the emotional transaction and the financial transaction take place, then I won't be able to be disturbed by it.'

VIII.

Speak to any artist who has exhibited at an art fair and they will likely tell you that while the conditions for display are far from ideal, participating is necessary if you intend to make a living. Speak to any gallerist and they will likely tell you their business depends upon it. 'The one thing that I would say that really makes sense,' Wine says of mounting a commercially successful booth at Frieze, 'is to be consistent in your display. Because it's the same as when you go to a shoe shop. You don't see a pair of stilettos next to a pair of Timberlands next to a pair of flip-flops. You don't see that. You see four different colours of Timberlands. Because then you've got a choice, but within a confined environment. And I think that's how the fair operates, that's why the people with the display which turns over the most cash – and that is obviously the goal of it – are the ones that fucking treat it as a normal commercial environment.'

London gallery Stuart Shave Modern Art is no stranger to the logic of the shoe shop. In 2015 it was declared winner of the Pommery Champagne Stand Prize, receiving as its reward £10,000 and a bottle of Pommery the size of a small child. On the walls of its booth were five works by artist Mark Flood, identically sized and evenly spaced in a range of colours, each a pixellated image of a Mark Rothko painting. Here, surely, is that *choice within a confined environment*, a reproduction of a popular product for sale in bubblegum pinks and greens, as well as deep purple and midnight blue for the more soberly inclined. And on the floor of the booth, a line of sculptures by Yngve Holen – seven washing machines, each topped with a warped sheet of plexiglass, and model aeroplanes pointing in various directions. The masterful control of minor differences – the choice between an aeroplane pointing East or West, of plexiglass bent upwards or plexiglass bent down – and of course the domestic scale they offered to Flood's Rothko's – useful as an indication of how they might fit in back home – ensured the stand was triumphant. No mention of the 'different-colours-of-Timberland-boots' approach was made by the judging panel, who praised instead the 'intellectual and formal dialogue', but one can only assume it had been tacitly acknowledged.

With the financial stakes so high for artists and galleries alike, and with certain types of artwork proving bankable, it doesn't take a huge leap of the imagination to see how the art fair has begun to dictate the nature of artworks being produced. This idea was given short shrift at Frieze HQ. 'Look,' Slotover tells me, 'I think it's your duty as an artist to make the best work you possibly can. And to follow your interests and your dreams and whatever.' But, 'if the gallery is exerting pressure on you as an artist to make work that you don't think is good, well, there's no gun to your head. It's your decision. If a gallery says, "Oh, I quite like that piece but can you make it smaller, and in pink, because we could sell it?" you've got a choice. Either you say "Great, I'd love some money this month, and if you think so, I'll do one in pink." Or you can say "How dare you tell me what to make. I'm off, I'm going with another who's not going to do that." Eventually, it's down to the artist. And all artists have to think about it. "Am I interested in selling stuff, do I want the market to follow me or me to follow it?"'

I ask Jake Chapman about the experience of exhibiting at an art fair, and he replies with characteristic merriment. 'When you go to Frieze and you see the scale of things, and you see the works in such a homogenised environment – in a sense you get to see how hopeless a work of art is, as a thing which can actually fulfil all of the things you want it to do when you're in the process of making the thing. And that's easier to have when objects can gang up on the viewer, when there are enough objects or enough paintings that can build some kind of cosmology of meaning based on their context. But when it's one thing, then another thing, then another thing, it's like watching the existential crisis of the work of art, not being able to actually get away with what it's supposed to do.'

Shorn of any affinity with their surroundings bar commerce, Chapman concludes, all artworks can be at the fair are 'little punctuation marks in someone's journey through this screaming forest of little existential objects which are just so totally orphaned, because their meaning is attached to context'. I recount this rather bleak appraisal to Matthew Slotover, who replies with an act of double-tracking *par excellence*. 'That's very good', he says. 'Did he write that or did he come out with that?' When I tell him it came straight out of Chapman's mouth, he is evidently extremely pleased. 'Really? That's excellent!'

... the entire private domain is being engulfed by a mysterious activity that bears all the features of commercial life without there being actually any business to transact.
Theodor Adorno

THE CHRONICLES OF OBRIST

A case study in looking busy

I once knew a goth named Emily who filled her home with tokens of the undead. She had a scalloped frill apron decorated with little pentagrams and skulls, and in her bedroom – among the neatest I've seen – scatter cushions were arranged at the foot of the duvet, each of them printed with cobwebs or embroidered with black hearts. During the weekdays she worked a nine to five at a recruitment agency, and her boyfriend came over two nights a week according to a fixed timetable, once on a Wednesday, and again on a Saturday, when they would order takeaway, watch the X Factor, drink exactly one bottle of chardonnay, and go to bed before midnight, him in a Nine Inch Nails vest, her in a pyjama shirt with the words SEE YOU IN HELL written across the chest.

Emily's possessions did not suggest to me a desire for the devil to feed on her soul, or for anarchy to descend upon her orderly home on the orderly terraced street on which she lived. They were objects in support of a script, props that served the purpose of reminding anyone she encountered – herself included – of the manner in which she intended to be known. It's a tactic that all of us have used at some point or other, either as a method of becoming, or of deflecting attention away from who we fear we may already be. The aspiring writer, who places a selection of intellectual books around the apartment before the guests arrive for dinner; the recently woke student, who counters his own fears of provincialism by calling out the shortcomings of others; the nervous lover, who lights a cigarette and composes the bedsheets to reveal her body just so, in order to appear the picture of nonchalance when her new girlfriend returns from the bathroom. All of us do it. It's just that some of us make for more compelling, and more successful, authors.

Before meeting the curator Hans Ulrich Obrist, I wondered whether the hyper-productivity for which he is renowned was also a scalloped frill stitched on to the apron of his character, a script through which he wished to be interpreted, where the supporting motifs were not little skulls or pentagrams or studiously revealed nipples, but networking, sleeplessness and innovation. I wondered, too, what this might say about the last thirty years in the arts. For if Obrist has been wearing that apron, he's been doing so on behalf of a sector baptised in the waters of 1990s Europe, a time when faith in the melding of private and public institutions was high, the promise of a profitable and progressive liberalism had yet to curdle, Tony Blair was still a Richard Curtis pin-up in the making, and one could still be forgiven (just about) for believing that the internet would be a momentous democratic leveller. Such a climate triggered what the critic David Balzer describes as 'an anxiety of professionialism' – a rush to adopt the language of 'work in progress', with the opening of so many art laboratories and project spaces, affirm the hipness of institutions, by supporting artists who made the museum the site of mini work-utopias – kitted out with kitchens, slides, reading zones and shower units, like proto-Google offices – and present a sector open and ready for business. Cue Obrist's entry on to the scene, a fast-talking, globe-trotting Swiss economics graduate, who spent his nights on trains, planes and office floors, installed his first exhibition in his kitchen in 1991, aged twenty-three, was appointed to the role of 'migrator curator' by Musée d'Art Moderne de la Ville de Paris two years later, and co-curated the first edition of the travelling biennial, Manifesta, in 1996. Here was a man who knew everyone and went everywhere, and who offered a brilliant example of what could be achieved by refusing to be cowed by physical and geographical limitations, and embracing the total collapse of work into life.

Obrist is an expert story-teller. So good, he's been a boon to journalists, whom he provides with a print-ready package of anecdotes and mannerisms. 'I believe a lot of things travel through rumours', he told me when we met in his office at the Serpentine Gallery in London, where he has been director since 2005. 'If you shift the rules of the game, you are more likely to produce a rumour, because it becomes a story.' If one assesses the rumours that fill the glut of profiles and interviews of which he is the subject, a sort of cultural Frankenstein emerges, part Joseph Beuys, part Mark Zuckerberg and part the Smoking Man from X Files – an ambitious, enlightened and disconcertingly well-connected European, and a man whose alien habits, while not always plausible, have become a form of popular entertainment. 'Hans Ulrich Obrist spent his teens travelling across Europe, sleeping on overnight trains and meeting every member of every art scene he came across', begins an article on the website *Huck*, retelling the now familiar tale of his early years. 'Along the way, he added so many business cards to his leather-bound address book that it wouldn't hold together.' 'I never cook and I never actually made a coffee in my life', Obrist once told the *Observer*, a nugget of lifestyle portraiture detailing the habits of the well-catered-to, notable here for the role it plays in the Chronicles of Obrist – a mythology of a man with so many places to be, so many people to meet and so much to achieve that he's engaged in a constant battle to open up new wormholes in the space-time continuum. Certainly this leaves no time for a kettle.

Key to the Chronicles is his often cited habit of drinking twenty, thirty or fifty espressos a day, depending on your sources, a method for accelerating productivity borrowed from the author Honore De Balzac, who fuelled his own prodigious writing practice with a reliance upon coffee that eventually killed him, and which, perhaps wisely, Obrist says he's subsequently dropped in favour of green tea. (For his part, Balzac did not take kindly to caffeinated pretenders. 'Many people claim coffee inspires them,' he said, 'but, as everybody knows, coffee only makes boring people even more boring.') Among the most popular chapters of the Chronicles is the Brutally Early Club, founded in 2006, which Obrist has previously described as 'a breakfast salon for the twenty-first century where art meets science meets architecture meets literature' – a Les Deux Magots in the age of Starbucks, a hot-desking, salon-cum-business meeting, where a who's-who of the cultural sector gather at dawn in twenty-four hour coffee shops. While it's hard to find out exactly what intersection of art, architecture, science and literature is so pressing as to require giving up the early morning, other details are easier to come by. '6.30 AM', it says on the club's website in red letters, highlighting, for anyone who may have missed it, that this club is hardcore. Beneath this, the destinations of meet-ups are listed like the locations of international fashion stores. London, Berlin, New York, Paris.

So popular are the tales of the Chronicles, that they can appear to supersede Obrist's more conventional curatorial output. Of the friends I canvassed by way of research, few had read beyond the blurbs of his many books (he says he aspires to write a book a day, and to buy one). All of them were aware that he has written more books and articles than any single human has time to, knew of some young artist whom he has made the subject of an industry crush, or else some young writer who has ghostwritten for him, that he travels extensively and constantly, and generally knew him to be, as the *New York Times* once put it, 'the curator who never sleeps'.

And so it was that when I arranged to meet Obrist at the Serpentine, I did so with an agenda, a wish to pry behind the scalloped apron, to see what I could find. I also arrived in the mist of doubt – a feeling that the script, whatever promise it may once have offered, had aged poorly. 'They say that the millennial generation will have more than five jobs in their lifetime. I think it's really exciting. I'm a blogger, a podcaster and an author', says the actress in an advert for Microsoft's Spectre Laptop – a young, blonde, white woman, sitting in a pristine, converted warehouse apartment decorated with bunting, tasked with selling back the privation of un-monetised leisure time, and a gig economy shorn of job security, as a desirable lifestyle with products to match. It was an advert that repeatedly appeared on my screen during the spring of 2017, and it reminded me of what that dream of unregulated, professional freedom has become for many. Another unaffordable laptop, another unaffordable home, and three jobs that barely pay.

I waited in Obrist's office while he finished a meeting at the Serpentine's Sackler Gallery across the park, passing the time taking in the view across Kensington Gardens, and making a cursory inventory of the room.

Desk: stack of books, *Mondialité*, by Édouard Glissant, Ulrich co-ed (hard to read, half content printed upside down)
Interior wall: print-out of cartoon tombstone engraved with message *R.I.P. email*
Far Wall: framed photograph of yellow post-it note – reads *OMG*

The framed photograph brought to mind a morning some years prior, when I happened to be seated behind Obrist at a symposium at a university in London at which he was a guest speaker. That day, I watched over his shoulder as he scribbled on post-it notes and fixed them to the black plastic casing on the seat in front of him. In the space of half an hour he had covered the casing with yellow paper scales, and around the lecture theatre, people craned their necks to catch a glimpse of this fantastical beast born of the office stock cupboard. Like many former art students, I have sat through a number of surprising lecture and seminar styles. Among them, the painting professor who switched out the lights and insisted the class listen to the Weather Report for forty-five minutes in the dark, in order that we understand why jazz is good and Tracey Emin bad; the man who prowled the stage barefoot in a patchwork flat cap, instructing us to loosen up, lighten up and produce automatic writing to the films of Wim Wenders; and the kindly but drunken lecturer who took the opportunity to nap when the image reel began. Such occurrences were par for the course during my time as an undergraduate, where the majority of the art history faculty appeared to have come unstuck from the present like a spent velcro strap dangling from an old shoe. What I had never seen was a lecture couched in the language of the corporate, and when Obrist took to the stage that day, he did so as an altogether different prospect. The post-it notes, the suit worn with trainers, the travel bag – all giving the impression, as one journalist put it, that 'he could be just another European businessman on his way to a meeting at, say, Adidas or Bayer' – had the surprising effect of ensorcelling a lecture theatre of art students with the promise of action and efficiency.

At the Serpentine, my inventory-taking came to a halt with Obrist's arrival. He stood in the doorway of the office for a while, fielding requests from staff members about a forthcoming lunch, and informed me that shortly, he would be obliged to take various urgent phone calls. The urgency of these calls soon dissipated (none occurred during the hour we spent together), and eventually he settled in the seat across the desk. We began discussing the reasons behind his famous resistance to sleep. 'I grew up in Switzerland,' he told me, 'and I was worried about the narrowness of the mountains. You couldn't really see the sea; it was visibly claustrophobic. I started to relentlessly work and seldom sleep. I came on the Balzac rhythm, and then I found the Da Vinci rhythm, which is more healthy. You sleep fifty minutes for every three hours awake. It means you sleep seven or eight times a day, and you're never tired.' The purpose of these experiments, he said, was 'rebellion, against the imposed homogenised time frame in which we are living, or in which we are all supposed to live – twenty-four hours, with eight hours' sleep, eight hours' work, eight hours' leisure.' As he spoke, he raised his hands in the air, and opened and closed them, like a person attempting to catch invisible flies. 'I wanted to break out of the rhythm imposed by society, and I'm still not conforming with it.'

I asked whether he considered his work habits as a model for other's to emulate, wondering what this might mean in relation to today's automatising imperative to be at all times productive and connected – whether logging how many steps you take in an afternoon, replying to work emails at midnight, or joining the millions of people compelled to take on night shifts, to make ends meet in times of austerity. It was a line of criticism of which he was aware, and to my surprise, he directed me to Jonathan Crary's book *24/7: Late Capitalism and the Ends of Sleep*, which takes aim at the encroachments upon sleep by state and market. The book begins with the example of the US military, who use sleeplessness as a torture method, while also considering it a goal for their servicemen. It goes on to detail plans to send satellites into orbit, for the purpose of reflecting sunlight back to earth, thus facilitating through-the-night labour. The logic is as simple as it is effective. A prisoner kept up for days will admit to pretty much anything, a soldier who can stay awake for nights on end is the ultimate war resource, a workforce available at all hours is a boon to profit margins. 'Sleep,' writes Crary, 'is an irrational and intolerable affirmation that there might be limits to the compatibility of living beings with the allegedly irresistible forces of modernisation.'

Obrist told me that he fully agreed with Crary's critique, but did not consider it applicable to him. 'It can easily lead to a misunderstanding, when all of a sudden the way I live, one would think that everybody should live like that. I don't believe that at all. I believe we should be free to come up with our own mix, our own rhythms, our own strange existences, *a la* La Monte Young' – the minimalist composer who, as Obrist explains it, decided after leaving school that his day would be twenty-three hours long – 'and that's mine, that's the way I work. I find it wonderful that now every second day La Monte Young just sleeps. He stays in bed. I'm very sympathetic to anyone who does that.'

Obrist is an advocate of strange existences. He sets great store by the customisation of his behaviours, which he tinkers with, like an engineer attempting to reprogram his own subroutines. During our conversation he referred to his younger self as an 'analogue internet', a rumour I had come across before – recounted by an acquaintance who works with him, and on the website of *South China Post Magazine*. (If one does even the most provisional of research into Obrist, it doesn't take long before various of his habits surface, the effect of which made spending time in his company rather like putting the batteries into a toy. Out came the familiar actions: the break-neck loquacity, the diagrams of conversations drawn on scraps of paper – our time together produced a biro cross, some half ellipses, and a flurry of dots – the stories of strategies devised in the quest for ultimate connectivity.) Like a search engine, the quantity of information he is able to provide, and the pace at which he is able to do so, is an indicator of performance. 'Certain artists flourish through hyper-productivity,' he told me, 'my work flourishes through hyper-productivity, the more links I create, the more productive my work is, because I make junctions, I make junctions between artworks, I make junctions between people, I make junctions between processes, I make junctions between hyper-objects, non-objects, quasi-objects and people, and junctions and junctions and junctions, and the more junctions I make the more junctions these junctions trigger.'

In spite of this lust for yield, over the years, Obrist has adapted his working habits to suit the needs of a growing career. His directorship at Serpentine has required him to drop anchor, and where he once travelled '365 days a year', he is now restricted to fifty-two weekends away – including Christmas, 'because I dislike profoundly this consumerist ritual of Christmas, which I don't believe in'. His approach to sleep has also changed. 'Initially I believed that we could basically do whatever we wanted, not sleep at all, or sleep every three hours. But then a researcher in Munich – I think his name is Roenneberg – he found out that we all have our own inner sleeping rhythm, and that inner rhythm isn't necessarily an eight-hour kind of rhythm. It might be sleeping two hours at night, and then having a siesta for two hours. For each person it's different. All of a sudden I realised that for a long time I had tried to force myself into some weird, absurd sleeping rhythm, and I needed to identify my own.' And had he found it? I asked. 'I sleep every night from midnight to six, seven am.'

I wondered whether this meant Obrist's days of experimentation were over, that the script had finally begun to change. After all, on average, Britons sleep seven hours a night, turning in between eleven and midnight. 'It doesn't mean necessarily that I went back to a *normal* kind of rhythm, because I then found all kinds of other tricks to play around with', he said, sounding, for the only time in our conversation, a little exasperated. 'Like a night assistant. So I have this night producer – he's actually now promoted to night producer – Max Shackleton. He used to work for me as a day assistant, but we found out that he cannot really function during the day because his sleeping rhythm is inverted. He can only sleep during the day and he can only be awake during the night, so then I thought, "wow, I will hire him to be my night assistant".' And what does Max Shackleton do, I asked, contemplating the man in the nighttime, paid to wear the insomniac apron on Obrist's behalf, now that it no longer suits him to do so. 'In London there is always something open twenty-four hours, so he does errands at night, he posts stuff, does google searches, all the things I don't have the time for during the day. The things I used to do before, when I forced myself not to sleep, are now done by him.'

A FUNERAL FOR FRANK BROOME

A case study in self-marginalisation

Frank Broome raised his long, pale nose aloft and inhaled deeply. 'What do you think?', he asked Kitty Week, the new manager at Broome & Faucette. Kitty twiddled the 'my Marxist-Feminist dialectic brings all the boys to the bar' badge that she had bought at a zine fair at Goldsmiths University the previous weekend, now pinned to a strap on her dungarees, and cast her eyes around the freshly painted gallery.

'You must be so pleased', she replied, admiring the way the light cascaded in from above where the ceiling had been removed, giving a sense of grandeur to the former newsagents.

'Game changer', said Frank, which was precisely what he had in mind.

Broome & Faucette had been running for five years when Frank decided it was time to make the step up to serious players on the London art scene. To do so they needed new premises. The old, small quarters above the train station in Peckham would no longer do. There were far too many art students and pop-up businesses in the area, and pipe-dreamers and vanity projects were not the kind of company that Frank intended to keep. Granted, it took the brains behind Broome & Faucette rather longer than their neighbours to reach this conclusion. Rough Arch, the only other respectable contemporary art gallery in the vicinity, had left the area three summers prior. Their founder had been smart about it, too, releasing a statement saying that she no longer wanted to be complicit in the gentrification of the area, and had decided to move to Soho instead, taking over a family-run cobbler that had gone bust after fifty years of trading. And so it was that on a bright day in early July Frank stood in the basement of Broome & Faucette's new home on Bermondsey Street, with an architecture firm for a neighbour, a reassuringly expensive baker across the road, and a lease signed, dated and filed in the office cabinet.

If Broome & Faucette was a little late to the moving party, it's fair to say that being *démodé* had long been its particular charm. Frank took pride in never using social media, and by the time he reached the age of thirty, he had grown liable to bemoaning the absence of 'real instruments' in contemporary music, and rarely touched a novel written after the death of Jack Kerouac. Yet he still considered himself at the forefront of cultural developments, and set great store by artworks that linked modern and ancient classicism to the present day. It was an approach that informed his fashion sense, in which antique watches, waxed jackets, futuristic trainers and the latest in Scandinavian rucksack technology were each something of a staple. It was also an approach to running a gallery that had proven to be profitable. Jonas Blass's carvings of plastic bags, sandwich cartons and take-away containers had been their biggest seller yet, and for the past two years they had pretty much single-handedly financed the gallery's operations. A collector's club in Little Venice had fairly hoovered them up. Five houses within a square mile each had a sandstone kebab box displayed on their sizeable kitchen counters, or granite refuse bags scattered across their lawns. Jonas's sculptures had even created enough surplus cash for Frank to realise a long-held dream, the publication of *métier*, a bi-annual journal of art writing and poetry.

métier had gained Broome & Faucette a small army of literary-minded admirers, young men and women carrying canvas tote bags bearing the names of obscure booksellers, and wearing spectacles that looked like they had been borrowed from an archive of 1940s optometry. It was little wonder it had been so popular, for a considerable amount of thought had gone in to getting the 'vintage clerk' look just right. Each sheet of paper was printed lithographically, and designed to look like it had been written on a manual typewriter – wobbly characters, uneven ink distribution and all. The contents was then packaged inside an old-fashioned cardboard document wallet, and secured with a length of nautical, blue-and-white striped twine.

But tastes were changing, and following Elvira Wokes's scathing review of -the-missing-link- in *TRIGGER*, for the first time in his life, Frank Broome had suffered something of a crisis of confidence. Truth be told, it was more than just his confidence that was at stake. Frank felt the profile of his entire identity quiver like a blancmange in a summer gale. -the-missing-link- was the last exhibition held at their Peckham premises, and it was Frank's pet project, inspired by the artist Marcel Duchamp and his notion of the infra-thin. How long it had been in gestation! How was it that Duchamp had described it? Infra-thin: the point at which body and object co-mingle, the moment at which the smoke from a pipe also smells of the mouth of the person who inhaled it, and best of all, thought Frank, the sound that a pair of corduroy trousers make when rubbing against the seats of public transportation. Frank began to see these micro-events as invisible but essential impressions of the artist on the world, labour at an infinitesimal and barely conscious level. Excited by Duchamp's chafing corduroys, he invited each of Broome & Faucette's artists to display the trousers they wore when working in their studios on the gallery walls. Damian Hassleback, an American painter who had been with the gallery since its inception, suggested they stretch the trousers over large wooden frames, so that each pair had the status of a canvas. Frank liked the idea enormously. Having recently spent some time with an architect selecting materials for the refurbishment of his house on Crumberwell Hill, he fancied himself as something of a wood connoisseur, and had the frames made from the same species of Danish Douglas Fir used for the shelves in the upstairs study. As for the trousers, Damian showed a blue boiler suit caked in oils, Jonas a pair of faded mustard chinos, Timothy Evermore his Kappa popper tracksuit bottoms, Jago Thackery his trademark grey flannels, and Barney Wheatfield, an old pair of Levi's 501s.

Frank felt a pang of pride looking at the trousers installed upon the walls of the gallery – five self-portraits of his most beloved artists, which captured in the various stains and worn-out knees all of the action and intimacy of their industry. There had been a wonderful turn-out for the opening night, too, and in that moment the exhibition had seemed a great success. But all the good feeling subsided when Frank was sent Wokes's review, which described -the-missing-link- as 'idk, about as fre$h as an old kipper in Boris Johnson's sock drawer', and called out the entire Broome & Faucette program for being 'pale, male and stale'. To make matters worse, Wokes's review had caused a stir on Twitter, and the two directors had been branded members of 'the old elite', and 'pretentious Etonian twats'. (Frank found this latter barb particularly unfair, given that he had actually attended Marlborough.)

The feathers of his business partner Thom Faucette were not so easily ruffled, but the criticism shook Frank profoundly. The problem was that he had always considered himself something of an outsider. Indeed, it was the very reason that he had been attracted to a career in the arts in the first place. He had certainly never wanted to work in finance like his father, or corporate law like his brother. At school he had hated rugby and football, and felt much more comfortable on the badminton court, and from a young age he had immersed himself in alternative forms of cultural production. At fourteen, he was the bass player in the grunge band *twisted ankle*, followed by a brief career as *MC Roach Rider*, and was renowned among his friends for his daring feats as a graffiti artist, spraying his tag, *BigBongz*, onto the side of the train tracks at Chiswick and at Kew. Later, while studying Art History at Bristol University, he had become a core member of the alt-folk ensemble *Planctonia*, arranging Beat poetry to the tune of Cornish sea-shanties. All things considered, Frank was horrified to be labeled an establishment man.

Over the spring, while the newsagent on Bermondsey Street was being converted into a gallery, Frank and his fiancé Clementine headed to Santorini for the first leg of a month-long sojourn in

Greece. By the time they arrived on the island, Frank's spirits had sunk so low that they spent almost the entire fortnight in silence, speaking only to place their orders at breakfast, lunch and dinner, and to make the necessary arrangements for boat excursions along the coast.

'*Ostrakon*', Clementine thought grimly one morning, observing Frank's sunburned face and dishevelled hair as he sipped fresh pomegranate juice on the hotel balcony, and nibbled, disconsolately, on the local salami. '*A man unfairly banished to the edges of the earth.*' (Having studied classics, she tended to view things from a lengthier perspective than most.) Understandably, Clementine was immensely relieved when their exile on the island ended, and they headed to Athens to stay with Frank's old university friend Orlando, and his wife Coco. The previous year, Coco and Orlando had decided to rent out their converted Huguenot weaving factory near Spitalfields Market and take up residence in the Greek capital, in order that Orlando could soak up the politics and culture on the frontline of the financial crisis, as inspiration for his latest poetry collection, *hellenic flEU*.

The change of scene turned out to be a resounding success. Coco kept a beautiful home and the apartment was a forest of pot plants, the parquet flooring dotted with artisanal rugs and unusual artefacts the couple had picked up on their travels throughout the region – casts of Minoan statues, amphorae and a particularly entertaining reproduction of Pan, which Coco was currently using to display her bangles. And, having written his PHD thesis *Paradise Queered* on the gendered connotations of Milton's inconstant use of iambic pentameter, Orlando was as well-versed as anyone when it came to identity politics. This was a godsend given Frank's predicament, for he recognised at once the nature of the problem at hand. Frank was suffering under the burden of toxic masculinity. It was a perilous place to be, and Orlando set about the task of relieving his friend of the unwanted load. If Frank felt uncomfortable with how he had been labelled by Elvira Wokes as 'pale, stale and male', they decided he would have to find a way to more happily define himself, and not be enslaved by the monikers thrust upon him. He encouraged Frank to attend to the wounds of his own identity, however deeply hidden they might be, stored away beneath his confident, clubbable exterior, happy home life and the overwhelming pleasantness of his social diary.

Orlando leant him *The Will to Change* by bell hooks, and he read it over the course of two days, lounging on a divan upholstered with a sherbet lemon meandros, and eating homemade sesame candies that Coco brought to him on a tray. 'In patriarchal culture males are not allowed simply to be who they are and to glory in their unique identity', writes hooks. Frank felt she was speaking directly to him. 'Asked to give up the true self in order to realize the patriarchal ideal, boys learn self-betrayal early and are rewarded for these acts of soul murder.' Hadn't he been coerced, all these years and with nobody enquiring with regards to his permission, into wearing the mask of privilege? A mask that was now impinging upon his peace of mind? He had not asked to go to private school, after all, and he had never been allowed to forgot the hullabaloo he'd caused at prep school for adopting what his mother referred to as 'common diction'. When he really thought about it, he was forced to face up to a long-held suspicion that he had been born into the wrong class. Frank for one was tired of being judged. If only, he opined, we lived in a society more tolerant of difference. When Frank finished reading hooks, Orlando recommended Maggie Nelson's book *The Argonauts*, and he was surprised to find just how exciting, and erotic, the nuclear family could be. On completion he declared to Clem that he wanted to be as good a man to her as Harry was to Maggie.

By the end of Frank and Clementine's stay, a buzz of excitement filled the air, and in honour of the mood of political awakening, Orlando and Coco decided to arrange a special dinner. Coco was a wonderful cook, and while in Athens she had embarked on a project of her own: a socialist supper club, with menus specially designed to reflect the subjects of conversation the guests had convened to discuss. Over the past six months, headline topics included 'Each

According to Their Need', where every attending guest was served a portion-size of venison calculated according to their Body Mass Index, and 'Collective Labour', for which the cleaning lady was given the night off, and the guests attended to the washing and drying of dishes as a communal activity. For this particular supper, Coco devised a brand-new menu: 'Eat Your Manhood'. The meal began with buttered asparagus bought from the local market, each spear chopped in two and poked into a ramekin of home-made tomato ketchup. Following this, she served aromatic octopus balls, and for the main course – an inspired, tour de force of political cookery – a large sausage decorated around the base with deep-fried nests of potato, arranged to give the impression of blonde pubic hair.

The meal was a great success, and when the last of the sausage had been eaten, a fresh bottle of retsina poured, and the beeswax candles bought that morning from the Orthodox Church had pooled upon the wooden table, Orlando clambered up onto his chair. 'In honour of my dear friend Frank,' he said, by now a little wobbly on his feet, 'I have invented an after-dinner game. It's called *Queerly?*. The purpose of the game is to help us to free ourselves from the straight-jacket of heteronormativity, and break out of the bondage into which we have all been born. Each time you play, somebody brings an object personal to them, and everyone has to think of a way to make it queer. Now, as you are all new to this, I have decided to take one for the team and put myself forward to go first.'

He jumped down from his perch and disappeared into the bedroom, returning moments later with an old school portrait of himself as a boy, wearing a woolen cap and a little grey jacket with red piping, which he duly passed around the group.

'Go on then', he bellowed, his cheeks flushed from wine and glee. 'Queer me!'

Frank was the first to try his luck. 'Well, you were so short back then. You weren't really a vision of manliness, if you know what I mean. You were also pretty podgy, and that ginger hair coming out from under your cap would have made you the target for some derision – especially if I'd been around. I don't imagine you had much success with girls.'

'I can assure you you're barking up the wrong tree there my friend', Orlando fired back. 'I'm not normally one to boast, but I was the first boy in the dorm to lose his you know what.'

Coco smiled. Orlando's combative nature was one of the first things that attracted her to him.

'On the contrary I think you were ever so pretty – feminine even', said Clementine. 'Your lips were coral pink, and your skin was as white as titanium. You almost look as if you've been painted, like the little princess in Valesquez's *Las Meninas*. I wonder if this could be a way into the queering process. Perhaps we could view you as part of the history of western art, of men looking at women? In this respect, we might be able to place you in the lineage of the objectified female subject, on the receiving end of the male gaze.'

'Gosh that's *very* good', said Frank, admiring his fiancé's erudition.

'Only one problem there', said Orlando. 'Ginny the school photographer was *most definitely* a woman! She was such a pin-up among us boys that we used to hold a rock, paper and scissors tournament before her annual visit, to determine which of us could be her helper for the day.'

Impressed by Clementine's effort, the group went back to the drawing board with added gusto, and a conclusion wasn't reached until sometime after midnight, when all of a sudden, Coco declared, 'I've got it! He's *cross-dressing*. But rather than a boy dressing as a girl, he is a boy dressing as an adult man – like an old-school business man, like his dad or something. He's performing an archetype, and in doing so, shows how ridiculous and unnatural that archetype is.'

Everyone was immensely relieved that Coco had finally cracked it – not least Orlando, who was saved the fate of being labelled a sexual failure – and with the queering process complete, the party turned in for the night, exhausted, but proud of their collective achievement.

The trip to Athens had greatly improved Frank's state of mind.

Indeed, he was so full with good ideas that by the time the plane landed at Gatwick airport in late June he felt himself a changed man. For one, he could proudly call himself a feminist. And, though he had not yet claimed the mantle for himself out loud, such was his awakening to his own, inherent otherness, that he felt a tingling pleasure at the prospect that he might, one day, declare himself queer. One thing was for sure: when Broome & Faucette re-opened, he was determined to show the world the real Frank Broome.

*

At two o'clock Thom Faucette arrived at the Bermondey Street premises, in time for the afternoon meeting. On the agenda for the day was the inaugural exhibition programme. As usual, Thom's presence made Kitty nervous. There was something about his sultry, intellectual brand of cool – ying to Frank's affable yang – that startled and fascinate her in equal measure. She had known him for going on four years, yet she couldn't remember him speaking a single word to her. His skinny frame, and the curious little gothic tattoos of dots and triangles on the underside of his forearm, only added to the mystique. Kitty watched as Thom's black, monk strap shoes crossed the threshold, taking in the tight-fitting suit trousers pressed at the front, and the pink t-shirt neatly rolled up at the sleeves that revealed the most slender of biceps. At the sight of his wan head topped with a beanie hat, her neck flushed a deep shade of maroon, and within seconds the colour had climbed up to her cheeks like an autumnal Virginia Creeper.

'Good to see you!' Frank said, slapping Thom around the upper arm. 'How's it going?'

Thom nodded and slunk back against the wall.

'Shame you couldn't come over last night. Clem made squid ink linguini, and we played an incredible game that Orlando came up with in Athens. It's called, '*Queerly*?'. The idea is, you bring an object that's close to you, and everyone has to think of a way to make it queer. Yesterday it was my turn and I brought my old teddy, Tiger. We went from bear clubs in Vauxhall, to not being afraid to show your vulnerability, to interspecies relationships. Anyway, it got me thinking loads about the narratives we get used to telling, and that if we want to, we have the power to change them, to present ourselves and our stories to the world in a different way.'

Without looking up, Thom removed the hat from his head, smoothed his hair backwards, and carefully stretched the ribbed wool over his skull so that his fringe poked out at the front in a neat quiff. Acknowledging his friend's interest – for Thom was a man of few words – Frank's enthusiasm for the subject grew.

'This is what I want us to talk about today, because changing the narrative is exactly what we need to do with Broome & Faucette. If we want to get good press coverage, we're going to have to do something politically on point. Queerness is something we need to tap into.'

'It sounds like a jolly good idea Frank,' said Kitty, 'but wouldn't you worry about presenting yourself as something you're not, taking up space that isn't really yours?'

Frank looked at her with kindly, patrician eyes. 'I had my doubts at first, too. But over the spring I learned that queerness means something different now. It isn't to do with who we have sex with, or even who we love. It's about discovering the ways in which we feel ourselves to be outsiders, and making space for that. Besides, running a gallery is about providing space, Kitty, not taking it. And after Elvira Wokes's awful review, we need to show a different side to Broome & Faucette, and take back control of our identity. Rather than pale, male and stale, we need to take our place among the marginalised.'

Kitty had to admit that it was an exciting new direction. Thom wandered off for a smoke, and with queerness in mind, that afternoon they thrashed out the outline for the coming programme. In the autumn, Timothy Evermore would show *big digger*, his latest hydraulic sculpture: the claw arm of a JCB, programmed to drag itself along and gouge a line out of the ground as it did so. Frank had previously imagined the work as an update of 1970s 'anarchitecture' – a history of daring men illegally unleashing power tools upon derelict urban buildings – for the age of artificial intelligence. After Athens, however, he realised he could present it differently, too: as a portrait of the loneliness, confusion and violence at the heart of modern masculinity. Following *big digger*, Jago Thackery would show *Hard Press*, a series of collages made from e-fits of criminals overlaid with wildflowers from an archive of Victorian botany. Kitty suggested they might frame the exhibition around the writings of Jean Genet, who did a terrific job of queering crime. 'This is exactly the sort of thing we brought you on board for', said Frank. Kitty was the newest member of the Broome & Faucette team. Orlando had suggested she get involved following the Wokes debacle, owing to her political nous – she had recently finished a PHD on the typography of lesbian separatist pamphlets in the 1970s – and her specialist knowledge was already proving to be invaluable. Damian Hasslebank's ambitious project, to make an oil painting of every one of the fingernail clippings cut off over a six-month period, was taking a little longer than originally planned. With a gap to fill, Kitty again showed the merits of her insight, suggesting that it might be a good idea to consider including some women in the programme. They settled upon inviting Ethel Gabor and Tamara Crayola, two exciting recent graduates from the Duchy Drawing School, to exhibit their work *Pompeii Porno*: a large earthenware piece displayed upon the floor in tiles, which bore the marks of an afternoon the pair had spent rolling around in wet clay.

Frank was delighted with the line-up for the next few months, but he was not yet satisfied that he had fully shaken the monkey from his back. To truly move on from Wokes's review, he knew they needed to do something that would really put a flag in the sand and signal the gallery's new direction.

'I have an idea', said Kitty, adjusting the pins that held up her long, scraggly hair into a nest on top of her head, giving the impression that a crow might land at any minute to commence the task of egg-sitting. 'What about Nina Silver? She did this amazing series of performances, *spells against my oppressors*, and they got a ton of attention. The Lyle employed her for a whole year, and every week she would cast a spell on the museum, calling it out for its flaws and binding it from repeating them. She covered everything from the extortionate cost of flapjacks in the café, the length of time it takes waiting in line for the ladies' loo, to the role of oil money in paying her salary. It became so popular that the Lyle even created a new complaints system. Staff and visitors could pop their concerns in a little box covered in rainbow glitter, and each week she would pick a problem to banish from the gallery with a magic spell. You must have seen it in the papers.'

Frank got out his phone and googled her name, and sure enough, a stream of news reports appeared. 'Queer Radical Artist Calls Out UK's Biggest Art Institution', read a headline in the *Daily Standard*. Beneath it was a picture of Nina's scowling face, adorned with peacock blue eyebrows, looking thoroughly unimpressed with the hand the world had dealt her.

'It does look promising, Kitty,' said Frank, a little apprehensively. 'But don't you think it would draw attention to things about us that we'd rather our audience forgot?'

'I can see where you're coming from', Kitty replied. 'But she is just the sort of person we want to be seen working with. And she offers all kinds of spells, too – we needn't ask her to start a complaint box. She recently went up to Glasgow to perform a warding ritual on the opening night of Modern Art's new premises in the docklands in what used to be a shipping yard, as part of a luxury development complex. Nina's role was to ensure that the gallery didn't participate in the yuppification of the area. Besides, the binding spells were really quite useful for the Lyle,' Kitty explained. 'Every time there was a dispute about poor pay, working conditions, or a lack of representation, she could cast a spell, and everyone would see that the museum was allocating resources to face up to the problem at hand. It was a way for the museum to own its institutional critique.'

'I see,' said Frank, warming to the idea. 'Why, when you think about it, it's like a new service industry. You get artists in and pay them to show you your flaws. And, in having them pointed out, they become a positive feature.'

'Exactly', said Kitty. 'Not to mention the fact that it will show we are on trend with the new fashion for witchcraft. Lately it's become really quite popular – it's a great way to associate yourself with the spirit of the historically persecuted and look good while you do it. While I was at Goldsmiths it was impossible to walk through the art department without seeing a student wearing a velvet choker, and next Summer, the ICA is putting on *Wiki Wikka*, a survey show that looks at radical-feminist witchcraft in the digital age. If we get Nina in now, it will show that Broome & Faucette has really got its finger on the pulse.'

Frank was always happiest when a new thought was brewing. Back at home later on that evening, when Clem brought his evening cup of camomile tea up to the study, she was pleased to find him brimming with excitement. His aptitude for new ideas was a quality that she admired in him immensely. Like a Beagle, she thought, he could sniff out the latest intellectual trends from a mile off, and once he'd got the scent there was simply no stopping him.

'Goodnight pudding', she said, ruffling his hair.

'Goodnight Clemmy', he replied. 'I'll be up before too long, but I want to get this email just right.'

That evening Frank stayed up until 11.30 p.m. perfecting an invitation to Nina Silver. He usually aimed to be as formal as possible in his exchanges, but given recent developments, he wondered if it was time to adopt a more casual, streetwise manner. 'Dear Nina', and 'Warmest wishes', simply didn't cut it, especially if he wanted to distance himself from the private school manners that had been foisted upon him. And yet, if he was completely honest with himself, 'See you around' did seem a little bit forced, and he couldn't bear the thought of signing off with 'Laters'. Eventually, he settled upon a tone that he felt suited him just right: friendly, informal – and as a last line of defence – potentially ironic, too.

Hey Nina

How's tricks? I'm getting in touch from Broome & Faucette gallery. This September we're opening our new premises in Vauxhall. We're keen to get our new home, and programme, off to the best start politically (and magically), and would love to work with you.

Would you be interested in performing a spell for us?

All bests
Frank
co-founder, Broome *&* Faucette

A few days later, a reply from Nina's assistant appeared in Frank's inbox.

Hi Frank

Nina would be happy to participate. She has some conditions that she insists upon when working, which you will need to agree to in advance.

The cost of the spell is £3,000
You will not disclose the cost of her services
Nina will be assigned an assistant by the gallery
She will need unfettered access to your offices, and all belongings in them, in advance of the spell
You will meet with Nina three weeks before the event at a restaurant of her choice
In addition to Nina's personal fee, you will pay for the framing of 6 prints
A firehose filled with red paint will be prepared and made available to use on the opening night

Frank was impressed by Nina's professionalism, and after a bit of persuasion, he managed to get Thom on board, too – with the caveat that the exhibition didn't feature Thom in any way at all. The publicity they would get, Frank said, would make the cost worth it alone. And so it was that three weeks before the new gallery was due to open, Frank arrived for lunch at Yotam on Islington High Street at Nina's request. He had nothing but admiration for her good taste, for Yotam was undoubtedly one of the most respected restaurants in London. Through the stacks of exciting salads and multi-coloured meringues, he caught sight of her peacock eyebrows straight away.

'Frank Broome', he said, darting out a hand as he approached the table, and regretting the formality immediately. Nina stood to greet him, and as she did, she revealed a long, white, mesh dress, through which a large black sports bra and matching lycra cycling shorts were clearly visible. On her legs a pair of white socks were pulled up over her knees, and on her feet she wore black sandals with chunky velcro straps – the latter of which reminded Frank of the orthopaedic shoes grandma had been obliged to wear following the surgeries to remove her bunions.

'I'll have the avocado shake', Nina said when the waitress arrived, without glancing at the menu. 'And the twice-cooked lemon myrtle chicken with wild rice salad.'

Over lunch they discussed what it was that Frank wanted from the spell, so Nina could get a clearer idea of how to prepare. Although it still pained him to talk about, Frank did his best to explain the 'PSM' debacle, and how he had subsequently realised that he had allowed an ugly narrative about who he was, and what he stood for, to proliferate. Nina suggested that what Broome & Faucette needed was a cleansing spell, something to get rid of the bad vibes that manifested in Wokes's review. Much to Frank's amazement, she also pointed out that his own, personal journey to self-acceptance was at the core of this process – that in the end, it wasn't really Broome & Faucette that required cleansing at all, but Frank himself.

'I warn you,' she said, after finishing the last of the coffee and walnut financiers, 'I don't take any prisoners. To rid yourself of negative energy and move on from this, you will have to confess to your former privilege, as a wealthy, white, heterosexual man. If you're serious about this, you are going to have to expose yourself, lay it all out on the table, show what it is you are leaving behind. From there, I can do the rest. It's likely that you will find this traumatic: the coming out process almost always is. But while burying your head in the sand may work in the short-term, it will end up causing you long-term damage. I propose that we call the opening night event *A Funeral for Frank Broome*, and treat is as way to say goodbye, once and for all, to the old you.'

Coming out. The words resounded in Frank's head, and the prospect thrilled and frightened him in equal measure. What would everybody say? Had they already guessed? Would they still accept him? Despite the obvious risks, he felt he owed it to himself to be strong enough to go through with it, and as he sent out the invitation to the gallery's mailing list later that week, he knew in his heart that it was something he had to do.

Dear friends,

We invite you to *A Funeral for Frank Broome*, where Nina Silver will be bidding farewell to patriarchy, heteronormativity, and privilege, and helping us to embrace a more fluid and radical tomorrow.

Please join us for wine and nibbles from 7 p.m. on 9 September at our new premises:
13 Bermondsey Street, SE13TQ.

Frank's resolve would be tested a few days prior to the opening when a courier arrived at the gallery to drop off Nina's prints. Kitty carefully peeled off the bubble-wrap, and propped the artworks in a line against the walls. Their content was certainly hard hitting. Three of the prints contained the same grainy photograph of Frank dressed in a three-piece suit, taken at his cousin's wedding a few years earlier, which Nina must have cribbed from one of his friend's Facebook accounts. The remaining prints each contained a single word: 'Rich', 'White' and 'Straight'.

On the morning of the grand opening, Nina arrived to make the necessary preparations for her spell. First of all, she needed to find some 'incriminating objects'. As requested, Thom and Frank were obliged to hand over access to their office, and it didn't take long before the material she needed came to hand. Inside Frank's wallet, she found a photograph of Clementine – 'a symbol of heteronormativity' – and on his bookshelves, a catalogue of Picasso – 'the last word in chauvinism'. In a drawer in Frank's desk, she found a Mont Blanc fountain pen, given to him by his aunt on his twenty-first birthday – as Nina sagely put it, 'what kind of prick uses a £400 pen?'. She also took the signet ring Frank wore on his pinky finger, given to him by his father, and the receipt from their lunch at Yotam which she found in the accounts drawer, and which she declared as 'evidence of a bourgeoise lifestyle'.

Having gathered everything she needed for the spell, she began marking out a large pentagram in the middle of the gallery floor, using a mixture of sea salt crystals, crushed rosemary and organic mixed peppercorns. When she had finished, Kitty placed an assortment of multi-coloured tea lights in a circle around the star, and positioned the repurposed fire extinguisher against the wall.

By 7 p.m., Frank's palms were sweaty with nerves. But as the guests began to arrive, he was soon comforted by the support of his friends and colleagues. Clementine's siblings Hector and Whizzy were there, as were all of the artists on the Broome & Faucette roster.

'Wow', said Hector, staring wide-eyed at the photos of Frank plastered on the walls. 'It's so *brave*, putting yourself on the line like this.'

Frank's parents had even shown up – albeit mostly out of concern, for they had already put the deposit down on the manor house they had agreed upon with Clementine's parents as a suitable location for the nuptials. There were collectors keen to see the gallery's new direction, and a number of Nina's own fans had arrived, too: art students dressed like they just escaped from a gym class at a clown school.

At 7.30 the gallery was full, and Kitty lit the candles around the pentagram. All of a sudden the over-head lighting switched off, and a whiney soundtrack emanating from speakers hidden within the walls drifted through the gallery. Obscure yet familiar, it reminded Kitty of a bad dream that lingers upon waking. A minute in, she recognised what it was: Alanis Morissette's 'You Oughta Know', only played in reverse. When the song ended with a screech, four actors planted among the crowd began to chant in unison.

'This is a funeral for Frank Broome', they repeated, until the audience fell silent. 'We have come here to witness the end of privilege. We have come here to cleanse him.'

As they chanted, Nina appeared in the doorway wearing a long black PVC coat, and a pair of lavender washing-up gloves. She held a tea tray in front of her with impressive ceremony, on which each of the incriminating objects was placed, along with a roll of clingfilm and a bottle of toilet-cleaning fluid. Slowly, she made her way to the salt pentagram. Upon arrival, she put the tray on the ground and proceeded to take off her coat, revealing her body, naked but for a pair of silver running trainers, and a roll of bandage wrapped haphazardly around her torso and upper thighs, with the word 'witch' scrawled across her chest in purple lipstick. The effect was electrifying. Whizzy clung to Hector's arm in fright, Frank's mother covered her eyes, and all around the room the guests were as still and silent as statues. As if guided by an invisible spirit, Nina closed her eyes and ran her fingers over the objects on the tray, before snatching up the signet ring.

'I present to you the inheritance of gold from father to son!', she boomed, holding the offending item aloft. 'Death to the inheritor! Death to primogeniture!' As she spoke, she set about tearing off a strip of clingfilm from the cardboard roll, and wrapping the ring in plastic. 'By air and earth, by water and fire, so be you're power bound, as I desire.' One by one she wrapped the objects, and when each had been placed within one of the five points of the star, she squirted the toilet cleaner all around her like an arsonist with a can of petrol.

'This cleansing spell is almost done', Nina said when the bottle was empty, rising to her feet. 'Of all the tasks that remain, there is but one. Please leave this gallery for five minutes, and take your belongings, too; you will thank me for this request when you see what I am about to do. The last act of this magic is to kill an unwanted ghost – the privilege that has haunted Frank Broome, our host.'

At Nina's request the crowd began shuffling out onto the pavement, until only Frank remained with her inside. Out on the street the assembled guests gathered around the window, and looked on in astonishment as Nina picked up the fire extinguisher and released an extraordinary shower of red paint all over the walls, drenching Frank from head to toe in the process. Once the extinguisher was empty, she chucked it on the ground, put on her coat, calmly walked out of the gallery, and headed off down the street. After a few minutes, by which time it had become clear that she would probably not be returning, the guests tentatively started to filter back in. When Kitty turned the overhead lights on, the gallery erupted into spontaneous applause. For on the walls, the photographs of the old Frank Broome, and those horrid words used to describe him, were completely obscured by paint, that dripped from every surface like the remnants of a massacre.

'Thank you, darling,' Frank said, as Clem cleaned his face with a wet-wipe, and handed him a glass of prosecco. 'I feel like the cloud has finally lifted.'

ACKNOWLEDGEMENTS

'The Pious and the Pommery' was first published by *The White Review*, issue no. 18, September 2016, and a version of 'Tobacco and Cedar' in *Dirty Furniture*, issue no. 3, September 2016.

Special thanks to Izabella Scott, a tireless reader and friend, who has improved practically every page of this book; Kristian Vistrup Madsen and Skye Arundhati Thomas, whose sharp minds remind me to get my own in order; Andrew Latimer and Harriet Moore for your faith and support; the friends, family members, pets and other acquaintances who have unwittingly ended up on these pages and who have not yet disowned me; and Melissa Hobbs, for sharing my track (the best gift of all).